Dear DAYCARE PARENT

By Jackie Rioux and Jo-Ann Parylak

OVER 101 WAYS TO IMPROVE YOUR CHILD'S EXPERIENCE

101

Illustrated by Heidi Graf

A Few Words from Jackie

This book is dedicated to the loving memory of my dad, Tim Shaw, who was always such a lively and fun spirit! And dedicated, also, to the memory of my friend Maryellen Avery, my first Director in this business. She taught me well! Finally, Jo-Jo and I would like to say a special thank you to my wonderful husband, Rob. Without you, this book would not have happened.

A Few Words from Jo-Ann

I dedicate this book to all the parents and children who have come into my life throughout the years. My heart has grown so much in knowing each and every one of you. Our interactions became the seeds of this book, so thank you. To my loving family and friends, thank you all for your support and encouragement. I love you all dearly.

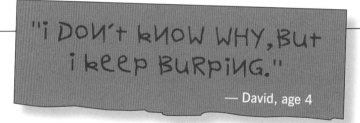

"i DON't kNOW WHY, But i keep BURPiNG."

— David, age 4

© 2016 Jackie Rioux & Jo-Ann Parylak
www.deardaycareparent.com

Attention Daycare Providers: Quantity discounts are available on bulk purchases of this book for educational training purposes, fund raising, or gift giving. Special books, booklets, or book excerpts can also be created to fit your specific needs. The authors are also available for Parent & Staff workshops. Please see our website for current offerings. For more information contact Dear Daycare Parent at info@DearDaycareParent.com

Publisher: Rioux Advisory Group, LLC
Website & Digital Services: Ingersoll Interactive, LLC (www.ingersollinteractive.com)
Design: Heidi Graf (www.mhgraf.com)

ISBN: 978-0-692-57249-8
Library of Congress Control Number: 2015919340
Printed by Versa Press, Inc. - Illinois
Printed in the United States of America

First Edition

Dear
DAYCARE PARENT

Date: 3/8/17

649.1 RIO
Rioux, Jackie,
Dear daycare parent :over 101
ways to improve your child's

TABLE OF CONTENTS

Acknowledgements

We would like to thank the many wonderful people we have had the privilege of knowing over our many years of working in the childcare field. There are too many to name individually, but you all know who you are! Many of the young children we cared for early on in our careers are now getting married and having children of their own. No, it doesn't make us feel older, just proud that we, like many others, had a part in getting their lives off to a great start. — Jackie & Jo-Ann —

Dear Parent,

Hi! We are your child's caregivers. We may have years of experience or just be starting out in the field. We come in all ages and sizes with different backgrounds. But, if we're here it's likely we have a love for children. We're sure not in it for the big money!

As a caregiver, we are perceived in many ways: to the children we are teachers, the mom, the boss, the friend, the kill joy, the nurse, the playmate, etc. To you, we are looked at as co-parent, servant, friend, psychologist, authority, information center, and sometimes even the enemy. Ha! No wonder we're so tired at the end of the day!

Anyway, here you are placing your child in our hands. It may take some time for us to build trust and understanding, but we share the common goal of making this experience a rewarding and enjoyable one for all of us.

So, you've made the decision and your "little one" is in a child care program either because of need or to provide him or her with socialization. This is certainly a significant change in your lives. Keep in mind that YOU are your child's first teacher and that role does not change when school starts. That's why it's important we work as a team. Maybe we'll even learn a little something from one another and be better for it.

Okay partner, let's go and enjoy this beautiful thing they call the wonder years, shall we?

— *Jackie & Jo-Ann* —

great (gr_t) *adj.* [ME. grete] 1. much higher in some quality or degree; much above the ordinary or average.

A GREAT DAYCARE EXPERIENCE:

As a parent you must have peace of mind when you drop off your child and go to work. You should feel well informed and comfortable talking to staff about any concerns. Your child should feel encouraged to learn and grow from their experiences.

In the pages that follow, we'll provide you with the information you need to make sure you and your child both enjoy a GREAT daycare or preschool experience.

— Jackie & Jo-Ann —

Taking Those First Steps

A SPECIAL NOTE FOR THE NEW PARENT WITH A NEW BABY IN DAYCARE

As your baby goes from your embrace to the arms of a new caregiver, you are overcome with a landslide of thoughts and feelings. This is perfectly normal!

You share the emotions of thousands of other parents who are parting with their infants for the first time, too. It isn't an easy transition, is it? Don't worry - you and your baby will be okay!

Here are a few things to remember as you begin this new experience:

First, go ahead and lean on the daycare staff. They are understanding people. Feel free to voice your feelings — no need to act brave — the most important thing here is COMMUNICATION. You will not look foolish if you ask questions.

Remember that YOU totally represent your baby since your child is unable to speak up for him or herself. You will probably need the first few weeks to be diligent:

- pay close attention to every memo and note;
- try to take a little extra time to chat with staff at the scheduled drop off and pick up times;

- observe the interactions between the infants and the staff, if something doesn't feel right, question it! Never feel like you will be offensive or that you are "burning bridges;"

- phone calls to the center and quick drop-in visits from time to time may ease your mind, too;

Along with all this, you have to keep an open mind and listen to suggestions made by the daycare staff. They are there for 8 hours a day managing and caring for not one, but several infants. Use them as invaluable guides to lead you to a better experience. You can learn a great deal from these professionals as they have experienced many different situations dealing with a variety of people.

In a short period of time, you will find yourself becoming more comfortable, more knowledgeable about this new world — and knowledge is confidence!

Throughout this book you will find general tips as well as tips specific to infants. We hope these will provide some comfort and make the transition to daycare an easier ride for everyone. You'll be a pro in no time passing your wisdom on to others!

Are You Ready to Roll?

Okay, so you've decided to enroll your little one in a program. Most likely, this is a first-time experience in a school-like setting for both you and your child. In this section we share some things you should keep in mind on how to prepare for that first day and beyond. It's natural to be a little nervous until you're comfortable with the surroundings and routine.

Before the Fun Begins

Here are a number of tips to help you get ready for the experiences ahead for you and your child.

#1 Ease Your Way In

Key Point:

Take the time to get your child comfortable and familiar with the new environment.

Summary:

Once you've selected a facility, visit a few times before your child officially starts. This allows you and your child to get comfortable with the new surroundings, the teachers and staff. This extra time taken before the actual start date will often ease the transition when your child sees you leave on the first day.

Why this is Important:

Children are often a little uneasy in new surroundings. Visiting a few times allows them to get used to the school. Your presence during a visit does two things: It allows your child to play and explore the new surroundings and, at the same time, still feel secure because they can look up and see you.

By stopping in the school, your child will be familiar with a few children in their class and feel more welcomed - and even feel comfortable enough to join in their play. This approach also gives you the chance to talk to the teachers while your child plays. When you feel more comfortable, your child will feel it and also begin to relax.

Real-life Example:

As is often the case, a parent came to visit our school because she was considering moving her child into a new program. As she explained, the director at the current school wasn't warm and often seemed short tempered. She said there seemed to be a quick turnover in staff and she was looking for a more welcoming school.

During her time visiting with us, she asked several questions pertaining to the staff.

- How long had teachers in this classroom worked?
- Where did we work prior to this school?
- How much experience did we have teaching?

While visiting and asking questions this mom started to feel more comfortable. She then asked if she could bring her son for a visit. She brought her son in the next day for a quick 30-minute visit while all of the other kids were playing outside during "outside" time. She then visited on another day after "nap" time. And then finally, she and her son visited a third time during the early morning.

By visiting in the morning and late afternoon, mom was able to observe what was going on at those times and see how the classroom ran. After visiting three times with her son, mom was sure this school was a perfect fit for her son, as well as their family. This parent truly had her son's best interest at heart and wanted him to be happy. When the day came that her son was to start, the transition was easy. He was eager to say goodbye and get involved with the other children.

> **"**
> *Children are like wet cement. Whatever falls on them makes an impression."*
>
> **Dr. Hiam Ginnot**

#2 Be in the Know

Key Point:

Each classroom typically has an area to post information for parents. Take the time to check the area to see if there is information pertinent to you and your child.

Summary:

This area often contains important information for the parents, staff, and even the state when they come to check up on the daycare. Plans for the day and the days to come are usually posted. If you have a question about something that is posted, you have access to teachers and staff right there and can address it with them immediately.

Why this is Important:

One of the most frequent comments we hear from parents is, "Oh, I didn't know." Communication is essential to ensuring a great experience each day for your child. E-mail has its place, but is not always timely. You, or your designee, are dropping off and picking up a child each day and should be checking the bulletin boards or communication area to see if there is anything you need to know. For example, if tomorrow is "bring a stuffed animal to school day" and you don't get the message, your child might be left out of the activity. No one wants that to happen.

Real-life Example:

So, what kind of helpful information can you find posted on those boards? Here are three good examples:

■ A sign in sheet that lets the staff know who is attending that day. The state will check these sheets sometimes to assure proper child/teacher ratios.

■ Lesson plans are posted so you can get an idea of what your child will be doing that week. It may also inform you of a special event or materials that need to be brought in for a project.

■ There may be news regarding an illness going around that you need to be aware of.

#3 Simply Ask

Key Point:

No question is silly. You don't know what you don't know. If you are unsure about something, don't let it bother you. Feel free to ask.

Summary:

Remember, this is your first experience in a childcare setting. You are not yet familiar with how everything works. If you witness an activity you think is odd or if you are not familiar with it, inquire. As teachers, we just go about our day and things are second nature to us. We often forget that there are times when parents have no clue why certain things are done the way they are.

Why this is Important:

Please don't walk away wondering or worrying about an issue. We have witnessed parents become disgruntled over the way a behavioral issue is being handled with their children. Instead of addressing it with staff, they will vent to other parents and that often leads to misunderstandings. If you don't feel comfortable talking to the teacher or staff, approach the director. And please don't think you're "burning any bridges" if you do this. Teachers and staff would rather you address the issue than not.

Real-life Example:

There was a little boy who said that his mom would yell at him for putting his coat on the floor before putting it on. What she didn't know is that is how he was being taught to put it on at school. Of course when we explained it she laughed. She thought her kid was just misbehaving and didn't think of asking us about it. It's really funny and kind of sad that as adults we are sometimes so afraid

to ask questions. On one Parent Night, the parents were given cornstarch and water and asked to mix it together with their hands and make it smooth. It was quite a while later when someone piped up and said, "Why are we doing this anyway?" We explained that it builds great hand and finger strength, which leads to stronger small motor skills. The new things you learn if you just have the courage to ask.

#4 Lights, Camera, Action

Key Point:

Be an actor. Children sense how you feel through your actions and expressions. Act and move confidently and be positive before you leave for the day.

Summary:

Children have keen radar and how you react to a situation can have a major impact on how they will react too. Your child will be closely watching your facial expressions and actions and taking his/her cues from your behavior. Keep in mind that you want to leave your child with the impression that they will be safe and happy in your absence, and that YOU are confident in the decision to leave them there.

Why this is Important:

Remember, you are setting the stage for your child's day. So whether it's your first childcare experience or you've been in it for a while, you need to establish a morning routine to make your child comfortable. And that routine includes being an actor and putting on a happy face even if you don't feel like it. Another way to avoid problems is to establish a routine that you use no matter how you feel. For example, enter the room with a warm hello and then check out the activities that are available. You may want to go over and get your child involved for a few minutes before stating, "It's time for me to go to work and I hope you have a fun day!" Some children like to sit with a teacher or stand in a doorway or window to wave. You don't want to show hesitation or keep going back as that can actually make your child feel like something is wrong. Always try to leave on a positive note.

Real-life Example:

We've witnessed parents get an angry face and say, "You better behave today or no TV when you go home. I don't want to hear all the bad things you did!"

Now what kind of tone did that set for the day? We know how hectic and aggravating mornings can be. There are days when the teachers don't want to smile either! However, we all need to be actors and set the right stage for our kids.

#5 Just Say So

Key Point:

Call or send a note to the teacher or staff whenever you have any questions or concerns. Open communication is one way to ensure your child's experience is positive throughout the year.

Summary:

You may find yourself wanting to discuss an issue with a teacher when you arrive to drop-off your child. However, because the teachers and staff are often in the middle of getting a bunch of kids ready for the day or engaged with other parents, you may find it difficult to actually get a moment with your child's teacher. This tends to happen as arrival and departure times are usually hectic periods in the day. A note or phone call may be your best option.

Why this is Important:

Communication is the key to any relationship. Don't allow the circumstances of a typical day to circumvent your desire to have a conversation. If the morning or evening drop-off and pick-up times are not conducive to conversation, find an alternative approach.

Real-life Example:

We don't want you to worry. There are several options you can take. For

one, you can ask the teacher if there is a time of day that would be more convenient to call or even come back for a chat. This is typically when the

children are napping or at a point when a substitute or staff from another area can come in to cover. We've also had parents keep a notebook in their child's backpack so that communication would be handled that way. This was usually when there was an ongoing problem that really needed to be monitored. And lastly, with today's technology some people will opt to make contact through e-mail. Most classrooms or centers are now equipped with computers. This isn't always the best though because there are days when things get chaotic and the teachers may not get around to the computer. We encourage important discussions to be dealt with on a more personal basis.

#6 Label, Label, Label

Key Point:

Label everything you bring in for your child. Use a waterproof marker. Everything from pacifiers, baby bottles, formula, lunches, and even clothes and blankets should have your child's name on them. This will avoid mix-ups and lost items.

Summary:

This is the one thing that we cannot express enough. Depending on the a-mount of children within each class-room, you can understand how easy it is to mix up the children's belongings when they are not properly labeled. For safety reasons, you don't want your child to get a food that may make them sick or that they are allergic to. So please clearly mark all your child's foods and put them in a special container that they can easily identify on their own.

Why this is Important:

For the younger children, many of the bottles and pacifiers look the same. For sanitary reasons, it is imperative that these items are clearly marked. As the children get older, they often have cups with characters on them. Since many children often have the same cup, the children will cry and argue over whose cup it really belongs to. As the children get older, they have easy accessibility to their own cubbies and some times may take a shirt or pants out of their cubby and then can't identify if it is theirs. If you don't want to label each piece of your child's spare clothes, then put the clothes in a labeled zip-lock bag. However, when it comes to outside clothing, it is best to label all of it. Often, the children's cubbies are outside of the classroom and the teacher doesn't get to see what the children brought in for outside time.

When a child has a brightly colored jacket or coat, they can easily pick out which one is theirs. But, if you live in an area that gets cold and gets snow, often the boots and snow pants are difficult to identify one from another. So, please put your child's name inside their boots, snow pants, and mittens.

Real-life Example:

One morning, a mom said to the teacher, "I just want to let you know Jessica has two main things for lunch, but I don't expect her to eat it all. We had pizza last night, but she doesn't always want the same thing for lunch. Just in case, I gave her some rolled up turkey and raw cut vegetables." When lunchtime came around, the teacher found the pizza in aluminum foil. She put it on a paper towel in order to heat it then returned it to the aluminum foil. The teacher took out the labeled container with the turkey and vegetables and laid it where the child could reach it to open it. When lunchtime was announced, one teacher followed the children to the sink to help with hand washing while the other teacher circled the table to help all the children open containers and packages that they couldn't on their own. All of a sudden Jessica says, "Mommy told me I could have pizza. I want that first!"

The teacher said, "It's on the table, next to your container."

Jessica said, "No, it's not."

When the teacher walked over to check, she saw that it was clearly gone, and the little boy across from her had pizza sauce all over his face. When the teacher asked him why he ate Jessica's pizza, he said, "Mommy knows I like pizza. It was mine!"

Children can't always identify food as their own and may eat someone else's lunch by mistake.

#7 Post It!

Key Point:

Designate one spot in your house for notes or information of upcoming events. This keeps everyone in your family aware of what is happening at your child's school.

Summary:

You may want to have an area in your home designated for notes from the daycare. Some parents have a special bulletin board they can tack things up on. We all have busy lives as we juggle work, family and other commitments. A central place where everyone can go to see the latest news is helpful.

Why this is Important:

At times, some families have different people picking up their child. Maybe mom drops the child off in the morning, but in the afternoon other arrangements have been made (Dad, Grandma, a friend or even a college student hired to care for the child in the afternoon). Because of this communication may not be translated correctly.

Real-life Example:

If we know about a special day before hand, we will often tell the parent ahead of time. For example, "Monday is Pirate Day. Everyone gets to dress up as a pirate" or "The children want to do Pajama Day on Friday." If you don't get this information or if you forget, your actions make a statement to your child. This says to your child that they were not important enough to remember - and their feelings get very hurt. No one wants that to happen.

#8 Getting To Know You...

Key Point:

Well-run facilities will request information about your child prior to the 1st day. You should make every effort to provide this information.

Summary:

No one knows your child better than you. That is why you may be asked to complete an information packet prior to your child joining the daycare center. Teachers and staff want to find out as much as they can about your child.

Why this is Important:

Your answers help the teachers learn as much as they can about your child to make the transition into the school easy and as fearless as possible. The information will be used to make your child feel more comfortable in his or her first preschool experience. Teachers particularly want to know things like: "What interests your child?" or "What makes them happy?" or "What scares them?"

Real-life Example:

Depending on your location, the questions may vary - but they always begin with general family information starting with the parent(s). Are you married, living together, single, divorced, separated, or are there any special circumstances that may be important. If there is a death of a parent or custody battle in progress, this is information that the school needs to know.

Other personal information or family information that is often asked include things such as:

Are there any siblings, pets, places you've lived, and languages the child speaks.

If your child is a baby or toddler, there may be questions about their speech such as: do they babble or is their speech understandable. Next, the questions will be broken down into sections like gross motor skills, emotional, toileting, and health. Here are a few examples:

1) Gross Motor

   a) What activities does your child enjoy?

   b) Do they tire easily?

2) Emotional

    a) Under what circumstances does your child become upset?

    b) Does your child have a particular fear?

    c) How does your child show fear? Anger? Frustration?

    d) What helps reassure your child?

3) Toileting

    a) Diapers: cloth or disposable?

    b) Is your child prone to rash?

    c) Are they toilet trained? If so, when?

    d) Does your child need reminders to use the toilet?

    e) How does your child indicate that they need to use the toilet?

4) Personal questions about your child might be like these:

    a) What adjectives would you use to describe your child?

    b) What is your child's favorite activities, books or stories?

    c) How does your child respond to older children?

    d) How does your family enforce limits and family rules?

    e) Is there anything special we should know about your family and/or child?

5) Under the section on Health / Medicine, are questions that let the school know if your child has any allergies, has ever been hospitalized, who is your doctor and dentist.

6) Does your child have any special conditions that would limit your child's activities that the teachers should be aware of? Does your child take any medications on a regular basis?

7) The last bit of information they ask is for an emergency contact person: the name of a person the school can contact just in case the parent(s) cannot be located.

#9 Great Expectations

Key Point:

It's not realistic to expect a detailed description of your child's day.

Summary:

Watching a group of children in constant motion is no easy task. As a result, it's nearly impossible to document what each child did during the day. The best you should hope for is a general accounting of the activity and an overall assessment of your child's participation and behavior. If you have specific concerns, simply ask the teacher or staff for guidance or for examples of your child's participation.

Why this is Important:

The last thing anyone wants is to start a new relationship with a daycare program and not have expectations met. When you meet with the teachers and staff, you should come away with an understanding of what to expect each day in terms of feedback about your child's day. If you think you're going to get a detailed written report, then you might want to modify your expectations. At most centers, this is simply not possible.

Real-life Example:

Teachers and staff will usually provide a brief comment at the end of the day when your child is being picked-up. This may be in the form of a note or it may be part of a brief conversation. In either case, if you have questions, ask the teacher or staff when they would be available for further discussion over the phone or in person.

#10 Sometimes Push Comes To Shove

Key Point:

Beware! Your child is in a larger community now and will experience such battle wounds as getting bit (especially in infant/toddler rooms), getting hit, pushed, etc. The children are just learning how to use their words and socialize.

Summary:

Yes, your child will experience some battle wounds now and then. They are in a large group setting and in close proximity to other children. Biting, hitting, pushing – these are all things toddlers do as they develop.

Why this is Important:

Manage your expectations. Don't be surprised when this happens. You need to know that these things will occur. Very rarely does one child hurt another so badly that children have to be sent home or to the doctor, but you should know that this issue exists. Your focus should be on teaching your child not to do any of those things and to also teach them what to do if it happens to them. You also want to understand the facility's policy on this behavior. Ask the teachers what they are doing to alleviate the problem – they should already have an action plan in place. For example, if a one year old is constantly biting, he/she needs to be removed right after the incident to a high chair or playpen and maybe be given a teething toy to bite on. And please take note that the caregivers will usually not share the biters name with you unless it gets to be a real problem. That can cause hard feelings between parents.

Real-life Example:

A grandmother of a 4 year old was concerned over little scratch marks her granddaughter had. Grandma insisted her granddaughter's classmates were doing this to her. Honestly it was just because she scratched herself on some equipment on the playground. Well, not believing this, grandma decided she would do some spy work on her own. She hid behind trees near the school when the kids were outside playing. She was intent on catching the little culprit who had scratched her granddaughter.

Needless to say, her outings proved fruitless, as she found no wrongdoing. Yes! Strange, but oh so true!

#11 | A Storm's Brewing

Key Point:

All daycare and preschool facilities should have a plan for inclement weather. Find out what the procedure is, whether it is tuning into a local radio station or waiting for a call from staff or other parents.

Summary:

Depending on where you live, you may have to worry about different kinds of weather issues: snow, ice, hurricanes, tornadoes etc. When your child is enrolled into the school you should expect to receive a packet of information that includes policies and procedures. Don't wait for a weather emergency to happen to figure out if your child can attend school. As a general rule most states require schools to be closed if there is no power or water.

Why this is Important:

If you live in an area that gets frequent inclement weather, such as snow and ice in the winter, know that the director

will be making the decision to stay open or close based on a lot of things. They will have you and your child's best interest and safety in mind, but will also consider staff members, too. In the event staff members cannot make it in or home due to a storm, plans may change. Due to state regulations, the director must keep teacher-to-child ratios in mind.

Real-life Example:

We recall one instance where a mom brought her child in as we were evacuating the building due to a hurricane warning. She was surprised that people were on their way out! All right then, guess she didn't notice the high wind

and branches falling. Anyway, during times of emergency it is always best to have your child with you, right?

#12 "I Don't Feel Good"

Key Point:

Have a back-up plan (such as a friend or relative) in the event your child is ill. Don't be surprised as illness occurs frequently especially when children are first exposed to other children's germs.

Summary:

O.K. so this is a biggie folks! This is a subject that childcare centers and parents clash over all the time. The bottom line is that you absolutely need to have a plan in place for when your child gets ill. Don't wait and then panic trying to figure out what to do if you can't get out of work. Perhaps a friend or relative can help out or you already have sick or personal time you can use. Sending a sick child in and hoping it won't be discovered they are sick is not an option. People seem surprised when their children sometimes get sick over and over in a short amount of time, but you have to remember this will occur especially when children are new to the program and are being exposed to new germs.

Why this is Important:

Children's immune systems are very immature at this age, and each time they do get sick it is a way for their body to build up more antibodies to

illnesses. However, in these early years, they do not have this protection and are susceptible to illnesses. Young children innately put things in their mouth, which gives germs easy access to their bodies. Be aware that your child will most likely get sick while at preschool, and schools cannot allow sick children to remain at school because germs spread quickly in this type of setting. You will need to have a backup plan. Give yourself several options, just in case you can't take the time off from work. Ask a relative or make arrangements with a neighbor.

Real-life Example:

One time a dad walked in with his 4-year old twins during a chicken pox outbreak, and of course, they were covered with little red dots. He tried to drop them off and make a quick departure, but we were faster than he was! As he exited with kids in tow he was trying to tell us it was just an allergic reaction. Are you kidding?

#13 The Small Print

Key Point:

Be sure you are familiar with all of the school's rules and policies. You don't want surprises down the road, especially if it creates an inconvenience.

Summary:

When you and your child are new to a school, you may feel overwhelmed with everything there is to remember about how the facility works. You will most likely get a packet that explains the school's rules and policies. And there could be a lot of rules and policies! Some will be simple, like when the school opens and closes. Others are more comprehensive. A few examples of policies you may find are:

- what constitutes a late pick-up and if the school has a late fee as well as how much it would be.

- what will happen if neither parent picks up the child, who is called if you can't reach a parent.

- what vaccinations your child is expected to have and at what age.

- If your child gets sick while at school, what symptoms they need to display in order to be sent home, as well as the earliest date they can come back.

- what illnesses are considered contagious and how long the child will have to be kept out of school if they get one of these illnesses.

- when the tuition is expected, as well as the consequences of unpaid amounts.

- if you want to take your child out of school for a period of time (for vacation or the summer), what will you have to do ensure your child's spot is held and whether or not you have to continue to pay the tuition.

Why this is Important:

Policies differ from place to place so it is vital to read information packets in order to avoid the "Uh-ohs" down the road. Daycare centers and preschools have policies and rules for a reason. Can you imagine what would happen if they didn't? There would be chaos. Most importantly, however, is that the rules and policies are for your child's safety. Everyone wants an orderly environment for every child. Following the rules helps make that happen.

Real-life Example:

We have been met with glares of disbelief when we have had to remind a parent that a child with a high fever may not return the next day. This is a common policy to prevent the spread of illness. And then there are the looks of dismay when a fee is assessed for arriving well after the center closes for the day.

#14 Let's Get Ready

Key Point:

You may want to bring in your child's supplies (baby wipes, diapers, bedding) a day or two before he or she is scheduled to start. This way everything is in place.

Summary:

It's a good idea to bring in any supplies your infant/child may need such as blankets, diapers, wipes, spare clothes, etc., a few days before he or she actually starts. That way the staff can have everything in place and everyone is ready to go! It's a more welcoming feeling too, like you are already part of the group. And when you think about it, it's one less thing you have to worry about on that first big day and you can just concentrate fully on getting you and your child situated.

Why this is Important:

You've spent all that time checking out your child's new school. Now it's time to make sure they are prepared. Regardless of your child's age, there are certain things that the school will ask you to always have on hand for your child. By bringing the necessary items in a few days earlier, it accomplishes two things. First, nothing is forgotten on your first day when you may be hurried. Second, there may be things that are needed "specifically" just for your child.

Real-life Example:

You may only be using cloth diapers for your child. You will have to work with the school to ensure that the soiled diapers go home. Or your child may have an allergy and this requires that your child have medication on hand. Prior to your child starting, the medication forms should be filled out and given to the school. Different schools require different things from the doctor. By getting this information a few days earlier, you will ensure that the school has all the proper information and that the form was filled out properly. Most schools have a nurse on staff that comes in and reviews these forms and it is not uncommon for them to ask for something to be clarified from the doctor for your child's safety and the school.

#15 Check Please!

Key Point:

It is important to pay school fees on time. Most centers are on a tight budget and depend on your dollars to pay the bills and teacher's salaries.

Summary:

Anyway folks, it's really important to pay childcare fees on time. Most centers do not have large sums of money available to cover expenses while waiting for fees to be paid. And it costs a lot to run a daycare center. In addition to staff salaries, there is the cost of running the building, and the cost of insurance! You all know what that is like. If you are facing financial difficulties please speak with the director as soon as possible. Things can usually be worked out before things snowball out of control like a child leaving abruptly and a large debt left behind.

Why this is Important:

Daycare is a business and businesses count on your payments in order to meet their obligations. In addition daycare centers also have to plan ahead for expected yearly expenses.

Examples of these are things such as: ground covering (sand or mulch), snow plowing or lawn care services and bulk art supplies needed for the children's use. The school's revenue is usually stretched as far as it will go. Therefore, when something unforeseen happens to the school, such as a major repair, it often puts a hardship on their finances

Real-life Example:

Ah yes, the joys of asking a parent if they have payment for the week. Approaching that subject can just be so uncomfortable! This one dad comes to mind who rarely paid on time, so every Friday we would go through our routine of me inquiring and him touching his pockets and wallet to see if the check was there, only to say, "I'm sorry, I'll get it to you first thing next week." To his credit, there actually were times he indeed would have his payment. Ha ha!

#16 Straight Talk

Key Point:

Your words influence your child's behavior. When you speak to your child during morning drop-off and evening pick-up times, make a consistent routine from day one. Children need routine. It lets them know what to expect as well as what will come next.

Summary:

We have one piece of advice that could make a big difference: be careful not to make comments in the form of a question. When you do this you are letting your child think there is a choice when there really isn't. Mommy HAS to go to work right now and we DO have to leave and go home. Examples of a

comment in a question form are:

- "Mommy has to go to work now, okay?"
- "Are you ready to go home now?"

When you do this, you are allowing them to make choices for you, and then they get upset when they realize they really don't have a choice. Instead, make your comments clear and to the

---

DAYCARE Did You Know

Studies prove that children who have rich early learning experiences are better prepared to thrive in kindergarten and beyond. (source: US Department of Education — Early Learning)

point. For older children, you can say, "It is time for me to leave for work now, find something to do." However, for younger children, who have trouble making a choice on their own, you can say, "You may join your friends, or you can start the activity that your teacher has set on the table. I need you to choose one."

Why this is Important:

Children need to know what to expect. It helps them feel secure. One of the easiest ways to do this is to establish a routine and be consistent. It is during the early years of preschool when your child's vocabulary has grown that they begin to debate, manipulate and try to control situations, whether that is in their play groups or with you. When children have a consistent routine they know what to expect and you will find you don't have to barter with them

> **"**
> *If you want your child to be intelligent, read them fairy tales.*
>
> *If you want them to be more intelligent, read them more fairy tales."*
>
> **Albert Einstein**

to get them out the door.

Real-life Example:

Just listen to these two scenarios involving two different dads we knew and how they approached going home. The first dad would come every night pretty darn close to closing and repeat over and over to his children" are you ready to go now?" to which they would respond by running around singing "no". This would go on until we firmly announced that we had to go and needed to lock up. Most nights we would wave good-bye as they were still fooling around on the playground. Now the second dad would look at his children and say, "let's move on outta here now!" to which the children would gladly run to the door. If there was a time they would say, "I don't wanna!" he would just grin and say, "It wasn't a question!"

#17 Manage Those Meds

Key Point:

If your child needs medication on a regular basis, or in case of an emergency, the first thing you need to do is make sure your daycare or preschool is willing to administer medications.

Summary:

If your child needs medications for things such as skin aliments or rashes, breathing treatments or just in case of an emergency (like Benadryl® or an EpiPen®), then you have to take the steps to get it ready for the school. The classroom might have more than one child on medication. Therefore, your child's medication should be separated and clearly marked. Put your child's medication in a gallon-sized zip-lock baggie along with any medication form or instructions. Write your child's name on the baggie and tape a current picture of your child on the outside of the baggie. The school should tell you how to label medications according to state guidelines.

Why this is Important:

Medications are an increasingly important part of life. You want to make sure that while your child is under the care of someone else, he or she will receive the proper dosage at the proper time and that there is no opportunity for confusion or for an error to occur. And with all of the peanut and other food allergies children have these days, it's now commonplace for schools to have an EpiPen® on hand for the more severe cases. If your child requires an EpiPen®, please be sure to send it in CLEARLY and BOLDLY labeled with your child's name along with the medical instructions provided by your doctor.

Real-life Example:

We have found it best to have a sign posted at the daycare with your child's name, picture, along with any allergies they have or medications they are required to take. This sign can be posted on a cabinet at the school so there is no doubt where the medication is located. It is also important to ask if the staff has been trained in administering medications and if not, who will be responsible. They should also be aware of the symptoms of anaphylactic shock. It is helpful if those symptoms are also posted somewhere in the room. Luckily we have never had to do this as we have been very careful with children who have severe allergic reactions. But it's good to be prepared in case of an emergency!

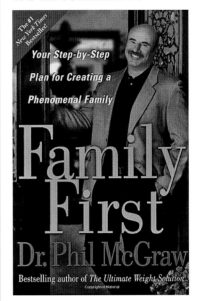

DAYCARE Did You Know

?

Twenty-nine percent of America's 4-year-olds were enrolled in a state-funded preschool program.

(Source: Barnett, W.S., Carolan, M.E., Squires, J.H., Clarke Brown, K., & Horowitz, M. (2015). The state of preschool 2014: State preschool yearbook. New Brunswick, NJ: National Institute for Early Education Research.)

What Every Parent Should Know

Our goal in this section is to provide you with some of the basics as you transition into a daycare facility. For many people, having a child cared for by others may be a difficult necessity. We hope to make it a smooth transition for you and your child.

These are common tips, not specific to any one area or time of the day. While these remain general in theme, they are very important to making sure you and your child begin your journeys on the right foot.

A number of tips in this section, as well as throughout the book, may seem like common sense. Believe us, if we didn't see it everyday for thirty-five years, we wouldn't have included it in the book. Sometimes it's the little things that make the biggest difference.

#18 Which One's Mine?

Key Point:

After dropping off your baby for the first time, you may suddenly panic over whether or not you will be able to recognize your infant when picking them up later on. Don't worry; this is a common phenomenon with new parents. Your baby's clothes may change throughout the day, but rest assured, you will still recognize your baby!

Summary:

All right, so you are probably laughing at this particular tip but it truly is a concern for new moms. Leaving an infant on that first day is particularly hard and very emotional! All kinds of thoughts start going through your brain whether they are rational or not. So please do not feel foolish. Ask questions and express your feelings and concerns. It will make the transition so much more comfortable!

Why this is Important:

In many daycares, you can enroll your child as young as 6-weeks old. So, when prospective parents come to visit we've heard them say, "Look at the babies. They are all so small and they don't have much hair. How do you

tell them apart?"

These same individuals have told us they fear not recognizing their own child when they come to pick them up. We reassured them that would never happen. They would always know the twinkle in their child's eyes, their child's smile or even their personality. Babies may have to be changed several times throughout the day. They spit up on their clothes or their diapers leak. But, no matter what they are wearing or how disheveled their hair looks from sleeping; you will always know your child when you see them.

Real-life Example:

After dropping off her baby for the first time, a mom panicked over whether or not she would be able to recognize her infant when picking him up later on. Of course, we assured her that everything would be fine and that she would recognize her child later in the day. And when she returned that evening, as expected she recognized her child instantly. We shared this tip just to let you know that these thoughts and feelings are normal.

#19 Just the Facts, Please

Key Point:
Baby and toddler areas usually have a special fact sheet designed for their age level. This sheet lets the staff know when your child last ate, how much they slept, and when they had their last bowel movement. These sheets are important.

Summary:

It's important to fill these out every morning so the staff has a better idea of what's going on if your infant is unusually fussy. Maybe it's because he or she didn't eat well that morning or had a rough night. Remember, you are your baby's voice here. In turn, the teachers will fill out the rest of that form for the day so you can have a good sense of what went on and take it from there!

Why this is Important:

The information you impart on these

fact sheets can be vital in caring for your child. If a child starts to fuss and they are not wet or soiled, the caregivers can use these sheets to learn if the child could be hungry or needing a nap. There may be times when your child didn't sleep well throughout the night because of a low-grade fever, or because they are teething. The more information you write down on these sheets, the better informed the caregivers are.

Real-life Example:

Imagine your child breaking out in a rash during the morning at daycare. It's happened. Usually it's because they were given a new food the night before. The sharing of information is the best way to make sure your child is given the best care.

#20 Make a List, Check it Twice

Key Point:
Check your child's supplies on a regular basis.

Summary:

This tip is pretty straightforward and needs little embellishment. At the end of the week, take a few minutes to check out your child's supplies. For infants these include diapers, wipes, and formula. Also be sure your child, no matter how old, has enough spare clothes for the week including socks and underwear. Simply jot down what you need on a piece of paper or your electronic device if that is what you prefer. Teachers will also usually leave reminders when something is running low. Don't forget now!

Why this is Important:

As a parent, you should get in the habit of checking your child's cubby (their personal storage space) on a regular basis to see what supplies they may need. We recommend doing this on Friday as it gives you the weekend to collect what is needed or stock-up. The age of your child will dictate what is needed. Babies require items such as diapers, wipes, creams or ointments, spare clothes, formula and food. Toddlers, who have yet to be toilet trained, may need many of the items from above. However, when they are beginning to toilet train, it is best to leave at least three sets of spare clothes on hand at all times. When children are learning to use the bathroom, they are not always aware of their bodily signals, which tell them they have to go to the bathroom. By the time they realize they have to go, it's often too late. For preschoolers, two sets of spare clothes are usually all that's required. We also recommend keeping some type of footwear and a sweater or sweatshirt.

Real-life Example:

There have been times that children have had an accident and the urine not only soiled their clothes, but also

their shoes too. By keeping some type of footwear (slippers, slipper sock, or flip flops) in your child's cubby, they will be prepared.

#21 It's Not Unusual

Key Point:

Don't be surprised if your child's behavior at school is different from his or her behavior at home. This is not unusual. Your child is learning how to socialize and act in different situations.

Summary:

During the early years, children are learning how to have their needs met and learning how to problem solve. This is all part of socialization. Conflicts arise frequently in classrooms where the children are very young and do not yet have a good vocabulary. It's not unusual for a child to exhibit different behaviors at school than those seen around the house or vice versa.

Why this is Important:

For young children, their idea of problem solving is to strike out such as biting, pushing or hitting, or just withdrawal. When an incident occurs, a teacher immediately intervenes. Many problem-solving situations become routine in school. The children see consistency from the teachers in how the situation is handled. Therefore, your child may behave differently at school than they do at home.

Real-life Example:

A prime example is when a toddler has a biting issue at childcare and the parent will say "but he never does that at home!" Not to worry, the opportunity to bite another child sometimes just doesn't present itself at home. Of course if this becomes a real problem you will be informed of actions that are being taken. Another common scenario is when a child gets high praise at school for clean up time and the mom will say that they don't lift a finger at home. Ha! You have to take into account that your child is learning how to socialize and act in different situations. So, no need to call in the counselor right away!

33

Key Point:

We totally understand how heartbreaking it can be to hear that your child is having a behavioral issue at school. If your child is acting out, keep open communication with the staff and work together to solve the problem.

Summary:

If you have chosen the right facility to enroll your child, the director and staff will work with you to find a resolution to the problem. Please don't panic or get defensive right away. Many places have a consultant on staff or have the resources to connect you with someone who can help. Very rarely does the decision to dismiss the child from the program have to be made. This only happens when all options have been exhausted and the safety of the children and staff may be at risk.

Why this is Important:

You've come to pick up your child at school and the teacher comes over to tell you about his or her day, as usual. However, this time when she talks to you, she tells you that your child had a very difficult day. He or she was yelling at the other children and was very physical. No parent wants to hear this about his or her child, but remember the teacher comes to you as an ally. By working as a team, you may be able to change this behavior. When children are this young, they are very influenced by what their parents think and do. By talking to and engaging with your child, you may be able to get to the heart of the problem and help change the behavior.

Real-life Example:

One child we knew would scratch the other children and often aim for the face. After more than a few children were being attacked on an almost daily basis, this was obviously considered a major problem. It's at that point that we needed to alert the parents to the problem and try to work together to come up with a plan of action to stop this behavior. Sometimes when talking with parents we discover an issue at home that can be causing the negative actions at school. Working together as teachers and parents can be very effective. In this particular case, however, we were following through with consequences at school, but the same was not being done at home. There were larger issues at play. Eventually, in order to keep the child in the school, the services of a professional counselor were needed. In the end, this move benefited the entire family greatly.

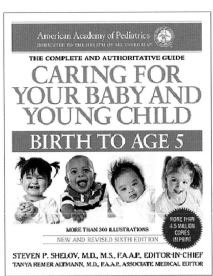

WE RECOMMEND:

American Academy of Pediatrics
DEDICATED TO THE HEALTH OF ALL CHILDREN®

THE COMPLETE AND AUTHORITATIVE GUIDE

CARING FOR YOUR BABY AND YOUNG CHILD

BIRTH TO AGE 5

MORE THAN 300 ILLUSTRATIONS
NEW AND REVISED SIXTH EDITION

MORE THAN 4.5 MILLION COPIES IN PRINT

STEVEN P. SHELOV, M.D., M.S., F.A.A.P., EDITOR-IN-CHIEF
TANYA REMER ALTMANN, M.D., F.A.A.P., ASSOCIATE MEDICAL EDITOR

Caring for Your Baby and Young Child, Revised Edition: Birth to Age 5 (Paperback)
By American Academy of Pediatrics
Publisher: Bantam

#23 Take Note... And Share It!

Key Point:

Read ALL the notes that are put in your child's cubby and make sure everyone involved in caring for your child is informed. These notes apprise you of a variety of things, such as: changes in scheduling, school closing, or even to tell you about a communicable disease that your child may have come in contact with.

Summary:

We are going to sound like a broken record here, and though it has been said many times, many ways, please read all notes that are left in your child's cubbies throughout the year! And don't forget to pass along the information to others in the family. These notes are important and are used to keep you up to date on the latest happenings. For example, a note might include reference to a form that your child's doctor needs to complete, or the note might tell you about an accident or an injury your child sustained that day. Maybe it's a million dollar refund! (Ha! Just checking to see if you are still paying attention.)

Why this is Important:

When there is something important to tell the parents (by the director or the teachers), often it is put in written form. This way, by putting it in a note and tacking it to the bulletin board, as well as, putting it in your child's cubby, it is more likely that everyone will get this information. Along with writing the note, the teacher's at the end of the day will also verbally pass along this information to whoever picks up the children.

Real-life Example:

A good example of this was seen one day when a dad came to pick up his daughter because his wife was out of town on business. When dad came in, the teacher informed him that there were two children in the classroom who had head lice. The teacher also told him there was a note in his daughter's cubby about what needs to be done if his daughter gets them. The next morning he dropped off his daughter and told the teachers that his wife would be back that afternoon and she would be picking up their daughter. Later that day when his wife came in she saw a teacher with gloves on looking through one of her children's hair. "What are you doing", she asked. The teacher explained that she was looking for head lice because of the two confirmed cases within the classroom. The mother asked, "When did this happen and how come we didn't know about it?" The teacher explained that a note went home two days earlier and that they also told her husband. You can imagine the conversation around the dinner table that evening!

> **"**
> *If you are always trying to be normal you will never know how amazing you can be."*
>
> Maya Angelou

DAYCARE Did You Know

? : On average preschoolers of employed mothers spend about 36 hours per week in childcare. (Source: U.S. Census Bureau)

STORY TIME

A little boy sighed and sat down to lunch one day. Before he began eating he just started shaking his head. We thought there was something wrong with his food, but when we inquired it was a totally different subject. He slapped his forehead with one hand saying, "Ai yi yi! Today is T ball, tomorrow is computer class, Saturday is karate, Geez! Can't I just stay home and play with my toys for once?" Out of the mouths of babes, folks!

#24 It's A Shoe In

Key Point:

Make sure your preschooler can put shoes or boots on with little or no help. Velcro shoes are an excellent choice. The preschool years are where independence and confidence begin to grow. Children want to be more self-reliant and are encouraged to be. Putting on and removing shoes is one activity that promotes self-reliance.

Summary:

As children begin to grow they take great pride in all their accomplishments! Even very young children feel joyful when they show you something they've learned to do. When you acknowledge their small accomplishments, you help them want to become more self-sufficient. Anyway, the point here is that the preschool years are where independence and confidence begin to grow and children are proud of the little things they can do for themselves.

Why this is Important:

One of the roles of a preschool teacher is to prepare their classes for Kindergarten. In Kindergarten, children are expected to perform most tasks on their own. Therefore, the preschool years are the years where they practice these skills: changing their clothes when they've had an accident, dressing and undressing for outside time, or even opening their own lunch containers, applesauce, yogurt and juice box. However, one of the tasks that children struggle with is putting on their own shoes or boots. Children this age are constantly working on their fine motor skills and finger dexterity. When they first begin to work on this task they sometimes get discouraged. They have to learn how to grab their shoe so they can hold it tight while at the same time push their foot into the shoe. When the shoes have ties on them, the ties often get in the way and hinder their progress. Adding to their frustration, tied shoes often come untied throughout the day. When children are wearing tied shoes, they often have to seek out an adult to untie their shoes whenever they want to play in the dress-up area or need to change their clothes.

Real-life Example:

Imagine a teacher practically standing on her head trying to get a pair of winter boots on a little boy. No matter how she contorted his foot into various positions, it just wasn't working. In the end, it was obvious the boy was in discomfort as the boots were from last winter and were now too small! And to add insult to near injury, the mom was upset when it was suggested that the boy needed a larger size. Really now?

#25 Dare To Share

Key Point:

Be careful when considering bringing your child's toy to daycare or preschool. When you bring in a toy from home, you may be setting your child up for disappointment. Preschool children are learning how to socialize. They don't share well and they can't be expected to.

Summary:

Since children spend a majority of their day in childcare, there are times when they want to bring in one of their toys from home. Centers tend to discourage this because the items sometimes get lost or broken. And at other times the child who brought the item in decides not to share and then the fights begin. Limit the items to things that are easy to share with the group such as tapes, books and CDs. These are things the teacher can put on or read for all to enjoy.

Why this is Important:

Very young children are very egocentric. They play by themselves and they believe the world revolves around their wants and desires. When the toys belong to the school, there is no sense of ownership, and therefore the children know the toys have to be shared. However, when a child brings a toy from home, they often feel as if they can make up all the rules regarding that toy. They will tell some children they can only look at it, whereas others will get to hold it or touch it. After a while, the child may become possessive and unwilling to share.

Real-life Example:

We had to put a stop to it at one point because people were letting their children bring in very large toys like castles and child sized stuffed animals. There were even breakable items making their way in. To solve this dilemma, we told parents they could bring in things like books, CDs, or games since the teacher could use these things at group time and supervise. We also had show and tell days where each child was allowed to bring in something special from home and share it with the class. If your child's school doesn't do this, you should suggest it.

#26 It's My Party

Key Point:

If you plan to have a birthday celebration for your child and want to invite children from school, send invitations through the mail rather than putting them in the children's cubbies. Feelings can be hurt when the whole class isn't invited.

Summary:

When you are planning a birthday party for your child, send the invitations through the mail. By doing this, it prevents two things: hurt feelings and lost invitations. When you put the invitations in the other children's cubbies, your child knows who got who got one and who didn't. Invariably, the topic gets brought during school hours and the children go to look for their invitation. The children that find an invitation are elated, but the children that don't find one are sad. Furthermore, the children who have found and opened their invitations do not put them back where you left them for the parents to find.

Why this is Important:

We know it may be hard to invite all the children to your child's party due to space, lack of extra supervision or just the cost. Often parents will bring in cupcakes on their child's birthday, but sometimes, parents have asked to have a simple party at the school so everyone can be involved. Talk to the teachers and see if you can have the party there. The children love special events where their parents are involved. Most schools are open to the idea. However, it is still your child's special day even if it's at the school. The teachers would expect you to be there, plan it, provide the necessary items and tell them what you want to accomplish. When the teachers know what you want to achieve, it is easier for them to block out an amount of time. Often with young children, the majority of the learning is done in the early morning hours up until lunch, when the children are alert and awake. So, when planning a party that has activities and games, keep this in mind. Just be warned, when you have the party at school, often your child will feel "this is their special day" and he or she will want to go with you when it's time for you to leave. However, if you are unable to take them home early, tell them the day before. Let them know that when the party is over mommy or daddy has to go back to work and they won't see you again until the end of the day.

Real-life Example:

At the beginning of every school year, most schools will pass out a class list. This list will have all the names of the children within the classroom, as well as their addresses, phone numbers and possibly the parents e-mail addresses. Please put this list in a safe place so you will have it on hand to make a play date, mail out birthday invitations or anything else that comes up within the year. After observing, participating in, planning and hearing about parties for children under five years old, we have to agree with the old rule of thumb: invite as many kids as your child is old. In other words if your child is 3 then invite 3 friends, 4 invite 4 children, you get the idea.

> **"**
> *Children are not things to be molded, but are people to be unfolded."*
>
> Jess Lair, author

#27 Off The Clock

Key Point:

After hours school functions are generally social events designed for parents and teachers to get to know one another. So please remember there is a "changing of the guard" and you are now responsible for watching your child.

Summary:

There will be times throughout the school year that the school may offer a social function, such as a "Meet and Greet" to socialize with the parents and each other, to view the children's classroom and see their artwork, or even a special dinner are examples of a few. There will be functions that are designed just for the adults, like events to help prepare your child for Kindergarten or a night designed to educate the parents giving them the opportunity to discuss any problems they may be having with their own child and get ideas on how they can handle these dilemmas. When the function is for the "parents only", it will be designated as such, but other than that, most activities are intended for everyone (parents and children).

Why this is Important:

During these after school gatherings, the teachers are no longer responsible for your children. In fact, in most schools, one of the policies in the handbook states that "when the parent enters the premises/building the teacher's responsibility for your child ends at the moment you greet your child". You will notice this when you pick up your child at the end of the day. The teachers step back and let the parents handle any behavior problems or other issues on their own. Some schools will have special functions designed just for the children at night. For example, "story hours" where the children come back to school after dinner in their pajamas. Other schools have offered celebrations, such as Halloween. The children come back to school in their costumes, play games, listen to a few age appropriate "ghost tales" and then get a small goodie bag to take home. Even though these events are intended for the children, the parent must accompany their child and keep an eye on them. If you see your child playing with toys, ask them to help you put things back where they belong. It's your child's classroom; they will know exactly where things belong.

Real-life Example:

One time we were holding a potluck dinner at the childcare center. Two older siblings were having a good time taking toys off the shelves and leaving them all over the floor. A short time later the parents declared that it was time to go and started heading for the door even though they were fully aware of the mess the kids made. Well, they must have been good mind readers! They took one look at us and realized what the issue was. They reluctantly returned to tidy up. There are no magic clean up people for after-school events. It usually falls upon the staff when the event is held at the school. So please be considerate and keep an eye on your child during these occasions so that everyone can have a good time.

#28 Don't Blame the Messenger

Key Point:

When the daycare calls to tell you your child is ill, please make it a point to pick your child up "within the hour". A sick child easily spreads germs to peers as well as to the staff. Every daycare has a sick policy and this policy must be adhered to.

Summary:

Ah yes! The dreaded phone call to the parent of a sick child who has to go home. We know it's not what you want to hear, but let's face it kids will get sick. This is when your back-up plan should spring into action. Telling the teacher, "she wasn't sick this morning" or, "I'm so busy at work" may be true, but it won't make a difference. The teachers and staff all understand that it's difficult to leave work or suddenly adjust your day. We have all faced that dilemma. However, the teachers are responsible for a room full of children and must keep the health of everyone in mind.

Why this is Important:

When a teacher notices unusual symptoms in a child, such as a runny nose, thick discharge, a low-grade fever or even a rash, they have to start monitoring this child. If the child has yet to be seen by a doctor, the staff has to assume the child may have picked up a virus. Viruses are infectious bacteria that enter the body and are very contagious. Viruses are very hard to treat because they do not respond to antibiotics. The longer a sick child is in the daycare, the quicker the virus will spread. If a child has been exposed to a virus, and that child coughs, sneezes, or touches something after touching their mouth or nose they are spreading the virus further. This is why the school has strict guidelines about when a child shows symptoms of being sick.

Real-life Example:

We will never forget the mom who was irate because she had to leave work to pick up her little girl. The child had vomited all over a teacher's leg and feet and was clearly ill. The mom argued with us and still would not acknowledge that her child was sick even though the "evidence" was in plain sight. Now, we all know the little girl didn't vomit on purpose! The poor child was sick and needed to go home. And imagine the teacher, covered in vomit, trying to convince the mom that the little girl needed her attention. Don't be that mom!

#29 What's in a Name?

Key Point:

Make it a point to know all the names of the teacher's in your child's classroom.

Summary:

Find out if there are others who interact with your child throughout the day. And if you see someone you don't recognize feel free to go over and introduce yourself. You can always suggest that the center provide a bulletin board with the teachers' pictures and biographies posted.

Why this is Important:

At the beginning of the year, most daycare centers will send out a newsletter letting you know what hours the teachers work. This way you will know which teacher you can expect to see in the morning when you arrive, and who will be there when you pick your child up at night. In addition, there may be other staff helping each classroom as needed or as a third person within your child's classroom. Either way, find out the names of the staff who will be interacting with your child and learn their names. If you need to call the school to let the teachers know your child will be out, or you are running late to pick up your child, or just you have a question for your child's teacher, you need to know which classroom your child is in and the name of their teacher. If you don't know the right name, then your message may never get to the right person. Also, if you don't know your child's teacher's names, you may feel uncomfortable approaching them if a problem does arise. You want to prevent this uneasiness, so get to know as many teachers as you can. There will be times when your child's class will be with other classrooms, like at outside time. During these times, you will begin to recognize the other staff members, but take the extra step to introduce yourself to anyone you don't know.

Real-life Example:

We had a mom and dad who were so involved in their jobs it was always a quick drop off and pick up. One day the dad approached Jackie to say that he knew her name, but not the names of the other three teachers who cared for his child. He and his wife were preparing to give us Christmas gifts and needed to know our initials. Wow! Don't be so out of touch. It's really important to know who is with your child all day, don't you think?

#30 The Needs of Many

Key Point:

The best way to manage your child's needs is to maintain good communication with the teachers. It's important to keep in mind that while the staff does its best to meet your child's needs, they have many other children to attend to at the same time.

Summary:

Of course every parent wants to think that their child is getting all the attention they need while in daycare. And yes we certainly try to do our best at spreading ourselves among all the children in our care. Just remember that it's not a one-on-one situation and some children need more attention than others simply because they have more behavioral issues, need more guidance, assistance, and redirecting.

Why this is Important:

Depending on the size of the school, the number of children in each classroom can vary in size, from as small as eight to even as high as twenty-four. When there is only one teacher, the main focus will be on the children and their safety. Although they want to welcome you and your child each morning or talk to you at the end of the day, they are likely to be more focused on ensuring the kids are safe and acting appropriately. If there is something specific about your child that you want the staff to know about, please verbally tell the teachers as well as leave them a note.

Real-life Example:

Take the case of the mom who insisted on calling us every day at noon to get an update on her child. If she didn't get enough information she would complain to the director. We can tell you, nobody wanted to answer that phone when it rang at high noon! Can you imagine if every parent did that? We would be out of our minds. So, here are a few things to keep in mind: First of all, when enrolling your child, be sure the classroom meets the child/teacher ratios. Also check to see if the program hires substitutes or floaters in case a staff person is out. Keep communication open by having brief chats with the teachers every day. Remain updated by checking email, reading notes being sent home, and checking any new posts on bulletin boards. Most programs nowadays also update you on your child's progress with written reports and conferences.

And last but not least, if you notice that staff-to-child ratios are frequently not being met you need to address that concern with your director.

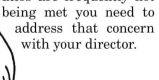

#31   It's a Professional Business

Key Point:

Working with children is a rewarding profession and both teachers and staff take their jobs seriously. When discussing a problem or issue with a teacher, please remember to address the issue professionally.

Summary:

Working with young children can be a very rewarding profession. We feel that helping people raise and educate their children is an extremely important job that is to be taken seriously. Keeping this in mind, if you should have any conflict or issues with a staff person at your childcare facility, please approach it in the professional manner in which it should be handled. In other words, don't stand there in front of other staff, children, and parents and yell at someone about an issue. The best way to handle any situation is to ask if there is a more private area where things can be discussed in a civil manner.

Why this is Important:

This tip was included because in our experience we have often witnessed parents engage staff members in a discourteous and demeaning manner bringing staff members to tears. There is absolutely no need for that! Whatever the issue is, do not let it fester; contact the teachers and make your concerns heard. Your issues can't be addressed if the teachers are unaware of your concerns.

Real-life Example:

We have encountered a few parents with whom we have had to put up our hands and state, "We'll be glad to speak with you once you have calmed down and can talk things over reasonably." And the same is true for teachers and staff; they should also demonstrate respect for you during times of distress. In the end, if you are not satisfied with the answers or the resolution to the problem, you should contact the director to intervene.

#32   Bright Ideas

Key Point:

If your center is offering or sponsoring a seminar, try to attend. It may be very helpful and give you new ideas. It's also a good way to become more familiar with parents and other members of the staff.

Summary:

We know, we know! The last thing you want to do after a full day of work is attend a class or seminar. However, your childcare center may be sponsoring a seminar or bringing in a speaker who may have some helpful and interesting ideas and thoughts on parenting. So, if you can, try to attend these once in a while.

Why this is Important:

Most states require that the teachers achieve hours of continuing education each year. And while we may grumble about going, there are times when we get some really helpful ideas to bring back to the classroom which could benefit your child. So maybe you could also walk away with some great information, too! And just so you know, the director will usually bring in speakers who are talking about an issue that he or she feels the parents could really use some assistance with.

Real-life Example:

We have seen first-hand the benefits of mini-seminars to guide parents and help them through some of the parenting hurdles. Most of them are open forums; each parent will come and ask a question about a concern that they are dealing with. This type of meeting is beneficial to all, because a question asked by one family may help another. Parents begin to feel that they are not alone in these types of situations.

#33 A Good Word Will Do

Key Point:

Running a school is like any other business. When you receive good service, tell someone.

Summary:

One of the nicest ways you can show appreciation is to tell a teacher you are thankful for the good care your child is receiving. Let the Director know too! The Director would love to know they have wonderful employees working for them. People are quick to go to the Director when something is wrong, but are slow to share the great things about the staff.

Why this is Important:

When you are happy with your child's preschool, spread the word. Tell your family and your friends, but most importantly, tell the people who are providing the care. This simple approach promotes the school and brings in more families. And don't forget to tell the staff. You may love their energy or the way they have made books and stories important in your child's life. You may have seen how warm, loving and compassionate they are toward your child. Whatever it is, tell them. Let them know that you've noticed and you appreciate them for it.

Real-life Example:

Frequently when people hear that we work in childcare they respond with comments like, "how cute" or "oh it must be fun!" With comments like these, it is clear people have no idea what happens in a daycare or preschool setting. Yes, the kids can be cute and there is fun involved, but believe us, a lot of work goes into having a quality childcare experience. And how should we delicately put it? All the children do not have halos over their heads. We take our work seriously and have to work hard at providing a safe and happy learning environment. And keep in mind we have to love what we do because we sure are not getting rich doing this! Our rewards basically come from watching a child thrive and grow. So, folks if you really want to give a big boost to a teacher's day, simply thank them for taking good care of your child while you are at work. It is appreciated more than you know.

#34 Keep That Number Handy

Key Point:

Keep the school's phone number with you at all times. You might need it to report an emergency, make a schedule change, or to discuss an issue with a teacher.

Summary:

You really should keep the number for your childcare center's number handy. And these days it's so easy to just include it in your contacts on your cell phone. You never know when you may have to give them a call, especially if you are stuck in traffic or are having car problems and will be arriving late to pick up your child. Keep in mind, the environment is a busy one and the teacher may not be able to take your call or stay on the line for long.

Why this is Important:

Life happens. We all face circumstances from time to time that require us to alter plans or make exceptions. And then there are the family emergencies. Whatever the circumstance you don't want to be caught without quick access to the daycare facility. If the situation doesn't require an immediate response, feel free to leave a message. If it is something the teacher can handle quickly and easily, they will often return your call right away. If it is a sensitive issue that you want to discuss, teachers usually wait until the children are at rest time to return these types of phone calls. This gives them more time to talk to you without interruption and no little ears will be around to overhear the conversation.

Real-life Example:

Unfortunately, we can tell you that there are parents out there who don't know the names of the people who care for their child, and who don't even have the number of the facility plugged into their cell phones. Even though there are times when we feel this society has become way too automated, this is a no-brainer.

#35 Allergy Alert

Key Point:

If your child has allergies, provide a large picture of your child with the words "ALLERGY ALERT" written on it and attach a list of your child's allergies. This helps prevent confusion should the daycare center have two children with the same first name.

Summary:

If your child is allergic to anything, especially foods like nuts or eggs, please be sure that there is a large sign in the classroom with your child's picture on it. Include a listing of all of the allergies your child has. It should be in an area where all the staff can see and be aware because a substitute, floater, or volunteer who is not with your child on a daily basis may have no idea and give them something they shouldn't have during lunch or snack times.

Why this is Important:

We don't know what it is, but the number of children with food allergies has drastically increased since we first began teaching preschool! There was a time when it wasn't even an issue at all. Because it occurs more often now, we all have to take precautions. For example, if your child is allergic to peanut butter, the teachers will know not to sit your child next to a child that has peanut butter for lunch. Or if they are doing a cooking project and one of the children is allergic to raw eggs, they will let that child assist with the project before the eggs are added in. If you are a parent of a child who is allergy free, it may be helpful to know what the allergies are in your child's classroom so that you can be considerate when sending in a snack or special treat.

Real-life Example:

We did have a child many years ago that had a disease and was extremely limited to only a few foods; if he even touched an egg he would break out into hives! He was definitely a rare case, but we had to take extra precautions with him and had to be aware of what other children around him were eating so we could situate him accordingly.

ALLERGY ALERT

#36   Don't Bug Me!

Key Point:

Head Lice is an ugly reality and because of the risk of infestation, most centers have a policy. If your child gets head lice, remember, they cannot return to school until properly treated.

Summary:

If your child gets head lice, remember, they cannot return to school until properly treated with a medication designed for this purpose. The product used for head lice can be bought over the counter. Often parents will look for herbal methods or other non-evasive methods to try to treat the lice. However, because head lice is so contagious, schools will not allow your child back into the school until proper measures have been performed and the lice are completely eradicated, including the eggs, and you can give verification of treatment.

Why this is Important:

Once head lice have been discovered, it is a daunting task for both the family and the school. All family members usually get treated as a precaution. When using these products, pay special attention to the instructions on the box. It lets you know how long to keep the product on to kill the bugs, how to properly apply it and even depending how long your hair is if you will need more than one box. The instructions will let you know how to remove the chemical and how to use the special fine-toothed comb to remove the nits. Nits are the head lice eggs that stick to the hair shaft. The hair has to be combed every 2-3 days with the nit comb for a period of 2-3weeks.

It's the school's job to check all of the heads of the children who have been in contact with the infested individual. Along with treating the individual, the families and the school have to wash anything that the bugs may have crawled into: hats, scarves, pillows, bedding, stuffed animals and dress-up clothes, anything the infested person may have worn or come in contact with. All the items have to be washed in very hot water and then dried on the hottest cycle as well. The lice and the eggs are killed when hot temperatures are used. Anything that can't be washed, must be bagged into plastic bags for two weeks or until the threat of recontamination is over.

Preschool's fear cross-contamination because the children play so closely, they sit and roll on the floor while they play and their cubbies are very close together. Once each child has been checked, the first thing the teachers do is remove and wash anything from the classroom that may have been infested. The schools make sure the furniture, rugs and floors are vacuumed well in case a bug crawled off the individual or a loose hair with nits fell out. Since the infested person is having their hair combed every 2-3 days to make sure all the nits are gone, and has to continue this for 3 weeks, the schools keeps vigilant. Don't be surprised if your child is seen scratching their head and the teachers look for bugs. If they find any bugs or nits, you will get a phone call to come pick up your child. You will have to get there in a timely manner; they are trying to prevent an infestation!

These are some common myths about head lice:

Myth: People often believe that head lice are something children catch in school. The truth is that head lice are commonly caught from family members and in the community.

Myth: People can get lice from pets. The truth is that lice can only live on humans.

Myth: Lice can jump from person to person. The truth is that lice have six legs and do not jump. They crawl from person to person by direct contact or sharing items such as combs and bedding.

Myth: Only dirty children get lice. The truth is that lice can survive under water; therefore the cleanest of children can still get lice.

Myth: Head lice prefer long hair. The truth is head lice is not selective and it does not matter what the length of your hair is. Long or short, clean or dirty, anyone can be infected with head lice.

Myth: If you use a treatment and kill the lice, you will be free of them. The truth is that lice lay eggs known as nits on the hair shaft. If you do not comb the nits out from the hair shaft, you may be re-infected because the nits hatch every 7 to 10 days.

Myth: A person is itchy because the lice are biting them. The truth is that the itch is caused by an allergic reaction from the lice saliva.

Myth: If an individual is still itchy after they have been treated it is because they are still infected with head lice. The truth is the person may be itchy for 2 to 3 weeks from the louse saliva. Unless any live lice are found, do not retreat just because you itch.

Real-life Example:

Interestingly enough, it was just brought to our attention that there are actually companies out there that will come to your home and assist you with lice removal! Who would have thought huh? Go ahead and look for these services by checking the yellow pages or plugging in lice removal in your search engine.

#37 Be Cool, Follow the Rules

Key Point:

Don't be surprised or offended if a teacher reminds your child of the rules while you are there. Sometimes when parents arrive, children will test the rules because they feel the rules no longer apply.

Summary:

If you know the school has a rule that the kids need to follow, please do so. Otherwise it can create tensions between you, your child and the teacher trying to re-enforce the policy. We of course realize that everyone is different and some are more, shall we say, free spirited than others, but there do have to be some guidelines set in order to have a peaceful, happy, and productive classroom.

Why this is Important:

If you see your child is breaking a rule, please step in and correct it. Otherwise, there can be a domino effect. The other children know the rules. If they see your child breaking the rules and getting away with it, they too will begin to act out. Also, if another child is accompanying you when dropping off or picking up your child, please watch what they are up to. Whether they are another sibling, a friend or a family member, you are responsible for them and they must adhere to the school's rules as well.

> **"**
> *It is not what you do for your children, but what you have taught them to do for themselves, that will make them successful human beings."*
>
> Ann Landers

Real-life Example:

We had a little guy who was not held accountable to any sort of rules at home and the parents were proud to boast about this fact. Ahem...anyway, we worked really hard at getting him to listen and this was so there wouldn't be total chaos in the room. And that's the point: with no rules you just have a bunch of children going wild. Can you even imagine that? The mom even told him that he didn't have to rest during naptime. Excuse me? So, this child was held to following structure all day and then Mom would show up and you know what would break loose. He would even jump on tables and scream! Of course a teacher would have to demand he get off and that his behavior was not okay. By allowing this to happen, the mom had just undone everything we tried to accomplish.

#38 Change That Diaper

Key Point:

While you may prefer to use cloth diapers for your infant, cloth diapers are not really appropriate in a day-care setting.

Summary:

Before we begin here, let's be clear: we are totally on board with saving the environment and believe in the importance of recycling! Having stated this, it may come as a surprise when we say that sending cloth diapers to childcare really shouldn't be your first choice. We only say this because it brings up sanitation and storage issues. When parents want to use cloth diapers, the school has to have a separate closed container "for each family" that wants to use them.

Why this is Important:

While you may prefer to use cloth diapers for your infant, cloth diapers lead to many concerns. First of all, they bring up issues of storage and sanitation. When cloth diapers are used, it is the parent's responsibility to provide a container for the storage of their child's soiled diapers. Given the limited space at daycare centers, finding appropriate storage space for soiled diapers is not always possible. When disposable diapers are used, there is a designated central location to dispose of them, usually a closed-lid container under a shelf, in a closet, behind a door or in the children's bathroom. This brings up a secondary issue, sanitation. Cloth diapers will not be emptied or rinsed out by the staff. They do not have an area to clean them. Most importantly, the teacher's time is devoted to the care of your children, not doing their dirty laundry.

Real-life Example:

Honestly we've only come across a few parents during our careers who have opted to go with cloth and they were welcome to do so. Of course there are times when this is a financial issue and it is more economical for the family to go this route. Just remember to send in a pack of disposables to have on hand in case of emergencies. Also be sure to ask if this is even an option before you enroll your infant or child.

#39 | Wash it Where?

Key Point:

If your child has a bathroom accident, please do not expect the teachers to empty and rinse the soiled clothing. They will usually place the items in a plastic bag.

Summary:

Of course when dealing with preschoolers, we know there are going to be bathroom accidents, especially with the newly toilet trained little ones. Most preschools only have sinks intended for the children's use; they are not equipped with utility sinks. So, if your child has an accident the staff will put their clothes in a plastic bag. Due to sanitary reasons, they cannot and will not rinse out the clothes.

Why this is Important:

If you come to pick up your child and you see your child is dressed differently than when you sent them to school, this will give you a heads up to look for a bag of clothes. Most likely, the teachers will pass this information on to you when they tell you about your child's day. Remember to keep the school supplied with plenty of spare clothes at all times.

Real-life Example:

We only mention this tip because, yes, there have been people who have asked us if we can clean their child's clothes a bit first. It just isn't practical in a childcare setting when the priority is to clean up the child and return to the classroom quickly.

#40 Puttin' out the Welcome Mat

Key Point:

Parents are always welcome to visit their child at school. If your facility discourages this, you should ask yourself why.

Summary:

You should always be welcome to visit your child at school. Now granted, there are some times that are better than others to stop by because you don't want to disrupt your child's day. For instance coming at naptime and waking your child up to say hi and then leave wouldn't be a good thing. Yes, people have done that! Also if you know that your child will have a total meltdown if you visit and then leave, then perhaps it's not a good idea. Use your best judgment.

Why this is Important:

We would all like to think we found the perfect school for our child, but you still have stay cautious and vigilant! Although most schools work very hard to follow their state's laws, hire the best staff and provide exceptional child care, we still see shocking headlines to remind us that not all daycares are what they seem. If you stop by your child's school unannounced and the staff act angry or nervous, you have to question it and wonder why. It may be something as simple as too many teachers out sick with the latest bug that's going around, and the remaining staff are trying to cover all the classrooms. However, if you are still left with an uneasy feeling, then you need to drop by more often without warning. Always trust your gut! And pay attention to your child. If they fight you about going to school, wonder why.

If you drop by and they are happy and playing well, then your mind can be at ease. However, if their behavior has changed, always question why.

Real-life Example:

Children seem to really enjoy when a parent stops in to have lunch. It's also neat for the parent as they can interact with the rest of the children as well and get to know some of the playmates and teachers a little better. And of course when parents have finished their visit and are walking out the door, we've heard, "I don't know how you do it, I'm going back to work!" Ha!

52

#41 Better Safe than Sorry!

Key Point:

Most preschools will close if they do not have water, electricity or phone service. While this is an inconvenience, it is done for sanitary and safety reasons.

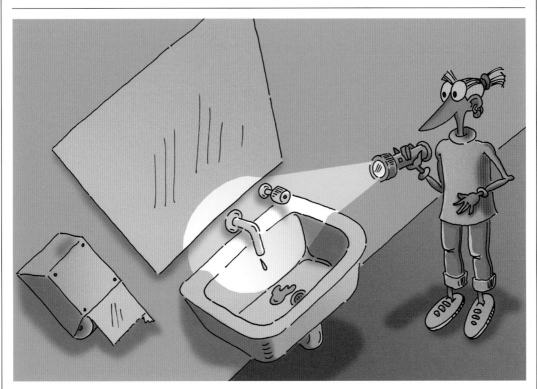

Summary:

Most preschools will and should close if they do not have water, electricity, or even phone service (cell service cannot always be depended on). As a general rule most states require schools to be closed if there is no power or water. The loss of phone service used to be in this category too, but with the onset of cell phones this is no longer an issue for many centers. If the phones go out, often the director will let the parents know that they will be using their own cell phone for the day.

Why this is Important:

Needless to say, sanitation reasons become very evident when there is a large group of children and there is no water for flushing toilets or washing hands. When the electricity goes out, it makes it difficult to heat the baby's bottles and the children's lunches. Along with this, not all the classrooms have sufficient windows to let in daylight. Therefore it makes it difficult for the children to play and move about safely. So, when the electricity or water goes out, schools must close.

Real-life Example:

We were truly amazed when our electricity (and therefore our heat) had gone out on one cold winter day just before we were supposed to open and parents were still dropping their children off. Inside the building we could see our breath as we spoke! On top of that we had no idea when and if the power would return anytime soon.

#42 Break Time!

Key Point:

Even though your child loves school, they still need some time away. Children need an occasional break from their routine.

Summary:

You know that as adults we certainly need a break from our work environment every once in a while. Otherwise we tend to get stressed or a bit irritable. Well you may not even realize it, but children need a break from their routine too! Think about it. They are up and at it early in the morning and have to go through the motions of the day at school. Some children are there nine or more hours a day. And guess what, sometimes they are just not in the mood!

Why this is Important:

Preschool may seem like nothing but play to adults, but for young children there are constant daily struggles and sometimes their spirits get battered socially and emotionally. As adults, you know how hard it is to deal with people and their diverse personalities. Yet, as adults, you have already learned all the social rules to make it easier for you to deal with these people. However, children this age, have yet to learn and use all these social guidelines. Consequently, there are some days that dealing with these kinds of social struggles leave the child feeling emotionally and socially beaten up, and it is evident on the child's face when their parents arrive to pick them up that they've had a hard day. Having a stay home day to recoup or a day of fun with mom/dad is often just what they needed.

Real-life Example:

We recall one child who was in the same classroom for two years in a row and did not get very many days off. You could see it was getting to him as he would respond to activities by saying "I don't wanna!" or "when is my mom coming?" Now mind you, his parents did take days for themselves, but there was never the thought that he needed a little time away too! Yes, they may love school, but why not surprise them once in a while with a little break? It can certainly be fun just to stay home in their pajamas and play with their own toys once in a while.

#43 Lay Down the Law!

Key Point:

Don't be afraid to correct your child's inappropriate behavior in front of the teachers. Using an authoritative voice and redirecting their behavior is important.

Summary:

If you come in and your child is acting inappropriately (such as hitting or kicking you), don't wait, you need to correct this behavior immediately. The staff will certainly not judge you, but applaud your efforts! It is quite often that kids will be fine until their parents show up and then it all breaks loose! So, if your child tends to do this at pick-up time, don't feel bad, it's not unusual. It's kind of a release after putting in eight or more hours at daycare. However folks, this does not excuse the negative behavior. We know it can be an awkward moment when both parent and teacher want to respond. You should know that the teacher feels that the parent should now take over the discipline.

Why this is Important:

When parents establish a routine for dropping off their child as well as picking them up and do not deviate from it, fewer problems arise. However, there may be times when your child had something happen at school with a friend or maybe you were running late and your child became frustrated, angry and upset. When you do not correct your child's behavior it has a domino effect,

they will revert to this behavior on the next time they are upset, because they had no consequences when they did it the first time. Also, when other children are watching this behavior in your child, they may mimic this behavior to their own parents.

Real-life Example:

We vividly recall a child who would just bounce off the walls when his mother showed up. He would proceed to break any rule possible. It got to the point where we would almost dread her arrival. There was one occasion when he jumped up on a table and when there was no action taken by her we had to strongly remind him that that was very inappropriate and unacceptable and had to physically remove him from the table. That mom needed to take charge, but she felt uncomfortable in front of staff.

STORY TIME

One day, one mom was telling a teacher that her job was so stressful lately that the next day she was taking a well needed mental health day to recuperate. She said she was going to drop her son off for school as usual so she could have the day to herself. The teacher understood and told her she hoped she had a wonderful day. The very next day, the phone rang and it was the same mother. She proceeded to tell the teacher what had occurred the night before: She said her son was playing on the living room floor while she was talking to her husband. She was telling her husband about her day and all the latest stresses. Next, she started to talk to her husband about how she was looking forward to having the day off tomorrow. Then she said her son, who was nearby listening, got up and walked over to her and slapped her. The boy then said, "Did you ever think that I'd like to have a stay home day too?"

The mom told the teacher, "Needless to say, that slap and comment gave me the wakeup call I needed. We chatted about there being better ways to get my attention without slapping me, but the bottom line is we are both having a mental health day, today! We'll see you on Monday."

#44 Dress For Success

Key Point:

When your child is going through the process of toilet training, please be mindful of what you are dressing them in for the day. You want clothes that aid them in becoming independent.

Summary:

Those t-shirts that snap at the crotch, overalls, suspenders, tights, or thermal underwear do not help in them becoming independent, and let's face it, these items are difficult to deal with when accidents happen. So, keep it simple with pull on bottoms. Sweat pants or other pull on pants are the best to use while your child is learning to go to the bathroom on their own.

Why this is Important:

When children begin toilet training, that is the beginning of their independence and they often refer to their new underwear as their "big boy" or "big girl" panties. While watching the older children go to the bathroom on their own, they too want to be self-sufficient like the older kids; which means, they need to have on clothes that can promote this self-reliance.

Real-life Example:

As you know, children tend to wait to the last minute and "do the dance" all the way to the bathroom! And it never fails that once we are all situated outside that is when nature calls and we must make a quick trip to the bathroom. Easy on and easy off is the way to go. So please keep all these things in mind as you dress your child for potty training success! Save that cute and fashionable look for later on.

Start on a Positive Note

Our goal in this chapter is to help you start your day off on a positive note. Mornings can be hectic and rushed. There are jobs to get to, things to remember, and events to plan or prepare for. There's a lot on your mind.

Routine is part of everyone's day including your child's. If you are rushed they will feel rushed and anxious – not the best way to start each day. One of the best things you can do for your child is to consistently begin their daycare or preschool experience in a calm and orderly manner.

#45 Turn Your Vehicle Off

Key Point:

Please turn off your vehicle and remove the keys before bringing your child into the building. Accidents can and do happen!

Summary:

While this may seem basic, it still needs to be said. Please turn your vehicle off when dropping off or picking up your child. Also be sure you take your keys with you. Why do we say this? Because there have been instances where a parent will run back into the school to get something and not only leave the vehicle running, but also leave the child inside. Oh yes, there have been older children who have managed to reach over and lock the doors and in the end the police have been called to open the doors! In the meantime both parent and teacher are holding their breath hoping the child doesn't do anything further!

Why this is Important:

We've witnessed it. A parent that is running late for work or to get home will pull into the school's parking lot. Then, with the car left running, they get out of the car and say to a child in the car, "Stay here, I'll be right back." Those six little words quickly get our attention and we keep our eyes on that car. But, it only takes a second for things to go badly. When children are young, they have not yet developed their cognitive skills. They are constantly working on their memory recall and they do not understand the consequences of their actions. They are unable to predict when they are in a dangerous situation.

Parents know the dangers of parking lots and no matter if they are at the mall, the grocery store or even at school; they can be heard repeating the same mantra to their child, "Hold my hand". Unfortunately, sometimes children have to suffer the consequences of their actions before they learn not to do something. We have seen unattended children get out of their seat belt (or car seat) and move behind the driver's seat, grasp the steeling wheel and pretend to drive. Bottom line, when you leave a child in a car that's running, they could cause a dangerous situation. Remember, safety first. Shut off your car and take all children into the school with you.

Real-life Example:

A mom came to pick up one child and left a younger sibling, who was ill, in the car. While waiting, the child in the car started fiddling around and CLICK went that LOCK button. When mom returned she became frantic at the sight of the keys dangling in the ignition and the doors locked. Soon fright came over the younger child's face, too as a) he figured he was in big trouble, and b) he realized he couldn't unlock the doors now. Panic set in all around. Other parents were trying to assist with ideas, one being the old wire hanger trick. Nowadays you are contending with the fact that cars have alarms, too. That lovely sound sure adds to the chaos!

After a while someone was successful in getting that lock up and was able to open the door. A couple things to remember here 1) not a good idea to leave a very young child in the car, and 2) ALWAYS take your keys!!!!

#46 Avoid the Great Escape!

Key Point:

Many schools have gated entrances for safety and security. Please remember to close any gates or doors behind you when entering and exiting the property. We wouldn't want any escapees!

Summary:

In light of the increased concern over security in schools, we thought we would throw this in as a gentle reminder. Most centers have gated entrances for safety and security and we know that sometimes your arms are full, or you are preoccupied, but please do your best to close any doors behind you. We certainly wouldn't want any escapees, as children can be incredibly quick.

Why this is Important:

When a child sees their parent's car pull into the parking lot, they will often run to the gate and begin pulling on it, as they wait for their parent to get to them. If the gate is not securely latched, the child can get it open. Once that happens, a child can easily run into the parking lot and be put in danger.

Real-life Example:

Once we had two mothers who had arrived at the same time and were chatting as they opened the gate. They continued to talk to each other, one mother had her hand on the gate, but she never latched it closed. We assumed even though she hadn't shut the gate and was chatting with a fellow parent, she'd remain aware and not let any children go past her. We were wrong. When a little boy saw his mother pull into the parking lot, he raced over to the gate, and pushed it open as he shouted out "Mommy"! The mother who had her hand on the gate looked up and saw the boy's mother and said without a care, "There's your mommy, honey." As she said this, the little boy raced past her and out of the gated area. The little boy's mother was just getting out of her car when she saw her son running toward her into the parking lot. The teachers were running to catch up to the boy and his mother was running to stop her son from reaching the parking lot. It wasn't until hearing all the commotion, that the mother by the gate realized her error. After that incident, the teachers learned a valuable lesson, they always had a teacher stand right in front of the gate to greet the parents and monitor that the gate was tightly closed after a parent entered and departed the area.

WE RECOMMEND:

No David!
By David Shannon
Publisher: Blue Sky Press
(imprint of Scholastic, Inc.)

#47 Penmanship Counts!

Key Point:

Most schools ask that you sign your child in and out each day. With many people coming and going, it is important to have safeguards and this is one of them! Please take a moment to do this.

Summary:

Childcare centers will ask you to sign in and out each day. We know it's not easy to remember to do this every time especially if your child is giving you a hard time and not cooperating. However, please make it a part of your daily routine. Every school will have its own way for you to sign your child in and out for the day. Some schools even have a two-step process of signing your child in for safety reasons. For example, some schools have a computer that you have to log yourself into, just to get into the main building; whereas other schools require you to punch in your personal code to get into the school's door. Once inside, you might also be asked to jot down your child's arrival time on a form designated as the "Sign-In" sheet; it is vitally important and mandated that you sign your child in and out whenever they are in the building. Signing your child in and out each day is done for legal reasons as well as safety reasons.

Why this is Important:

The state authorities use these sign–in forms to check to see if the schools are following all protocols and guidelines and are in compliance with the child/ teacher ratios for each classroom and age group. The simple act of signing your child in each day is important because it helps the State to monitor the schools closely, but more importantly it is vital that you sign your child in and out for safety reasons. As a safety precaution, once all the children have arrived for the day, the teachers will take a head count so they know how many children they have in their care. During an emergency, they immediately move all the children to safety and then take another head count. If this count is off, they quickly look to the parent's sign-in sheet to verify each name on the list. If someone doesn't sign their child in that morning, it becomes a race against time to figure out who is missing.

Real-life Example:

We have seen court cases where the sign-in information has been used to determine whether or not a child was dropped off in the morning. In one particular case a woman claimed that she had dropped her child off, but when the records were subpoenaed, it was discovered that her child was not in attendance that day.

#48 Read All About It!

Key Point:

Bulletin boards are posted either in your child's classroom or just outside of it. This board highlights important notices or information. Please read them daily.

Summary:

There are usually bulletin boards situated either inside your child's room or right outside the doorway. They are not just there for decoration so please take a minute when you enter or on the way out to read them. You will find such things as sign in sheets, snack lists, weekly plans, and notes from the director, weekly newsletters or even alerts about an illness going around the facility. Basically, this board highlights important notices and information you may need to have.

Why this is Important:

These bulletin boards are essential; they have an abundance of information that will help you and inform you of anything that you need to know. If there is an outbreak of something contagious going around in the school (such as head lice or chicken pox for example), a note will be put in your child's cubby, but it will also be announced on the bulletin board too, just in case the note in your child's cubby gets lost or overlooked. With the onset of the computer age, important information such as outbreaks is also sent through the Internet. Since everyone doesn't have accesses to a computer, the school tries to make it easier for everyone to get important information. That is why the

bulletin board is still their main source of information.

Lastly, by reading the bulletin board you will also have an idea of what your child did in school that day and you will be better prepared to talk to them about their day.

Real-life Example:

Now, we can't tell you how many times parents have come in saying, "I had no idea" about such things as upcoming field trips or special activities in the room. We finally took extreme measures and hung a sign from the ceiling so that everyone would walk right into it. Ha! People finally got the hint and were a bit more attentive. We realize that you are in a rush some days, but please try to take a minute when you are entering or exiting to read the board and remain well informed.

#49 Avoid Morning Mayhem

Key Point:

Many parents prepare their child's things the night before to avoid the morning rush. If you're rushing around every day it will be stressful for you as well as your child.

Summary:

With the busy lives we all lead it is no wonder that we're always forgetting things as we are rushing out the door in the morning. Mornings can be very chaotic. Parents are trying to shower and dress, prepare breakfast, collect the things they need for their day, as well as for their children. We have found that the parents who were more organized and planned ahead made their mornings run more smoothly and there was no disappointment for forgotten things.

Why this is Important:

Preschools always post (or e-mail) the

following week's lesson plan. Often parents will use a highlighter to emphasize the things they need to prepare for and have it ready the night before. Some schools will have special fun days or days that they'd like to teach a concept. For instance, they may have Color Day (asking the children to wear the color of the day), Dr. Seuss Day (reading his books that rhyme), Pajama Day (wear your pajama's to school), Pirate Day (dress like a pirate) or Hat Day, to name a few. There have been times when parents have forgotten or didn't prepare ahead of time and then when they came to school they realized that their child was unprepared for the day and they didn't have time to go home (to get what they needed or to change their clothes). Instead, their child started their morning feeling very sad. Make it a priority to look at the following week lesson plan, so you will be prepared and your child won't feel left out. To some parents, preschool is only a place they bring their child while they go to work. Whereas to other parents, they know that preschool will be their child's very first learning experience and they want to do everything they can do to make it better for them. Which group do you fall into?

Real-life Example:

Many parents have told us that in order to avoid total chaos in the morning they try to get most of their child's things ready the night before. Preparing lunches and getting supplies and belongings ready to go makes for smoother sailing the next day. It also prevents the important things from being left behind. How many times a child has cried because a pacifier or special nap blanket or sleeping buddy has been forgotten. It can just blow the day!

#50 What's Going On?

Key Point:

Keep your child's teacher informed of any significant changes in your life. It will help them understand any unusual behavior in your child.

Summary:

If you are told that your child is exhibiting unusual behavior at school be sure to reflect on what is going on in your own life. Some things that are happening at home may not seem important to you, but may affect your child's whole day. If something significant has happened it may be causing anxiety in your child causing him/her to act out. Kids are so sensitive to things even though you think you may be successfully keeping something from them. They can pick up on change in moods and routine.

Why this is Important:

When something happens at home, please take the time to let the teachers know. Maybe you had to bring your beloved pet to the vet, or you spent the night at the hospital with one of your children that have asthma, or maybe a relative has passed away. Whatever is happening in your life let the teacher's know. Even if you haven't talked it over with your child, they often sense when something is wrong or when something is different. Your child internalizes these events and may not always vocalize how they are feeling. Instead it is often noticed first in their behavior and then the teachers are at a loss to why they are acting out or just plain acting differently.

Real-life Example:

We had a happy and outgoing little girl who suddenly developed a crippling fear of a parent who used to pick up his daughter at the end of the day. It got to the point where she would cower in the corner right after she arrived anticipating the end of the day. Together with the parents we tried to figure out what was at the root of it all, but never did. One day it was just no longer an issue. It's important to remember during these times that a little extra TLC can go a long way toward helping a child resolve these stressful issues. You never know how these little minds are translating situations they encounter in their daily lives. What seems silly to an adult can be a major ordeal for a child.

#51 Bueller? Beuller?

Key Point:

Please inform us of any changes in your schedule (i.e. going out of town for business or family matters). Illness, injury, and general life events happen, even to kids. Let us know whom we should contact if needed.

Summary:

O.K. so we know there are times when you may want to play "hooky" and take a little time out for yourselves (just like Ferris Bueller!). Or maybe you just need to attend to some business and you can't bring your child. That is fine as long as you let us know that you cannot be reached at your usual location and may not be available to answer your cell phone. We need an alternate person who can be easily reached in case of an emergency.

Why this is Important:

We know that your lives are busy trying to balance the needs of your family, your career and your relationships; and due to this, most people keep a tight schedule to accomplish it all. However at times, life events occur and it disturbs your well-ordered routine. Whatever the situation, please let your child's school know, they will be more understanding if all of a sudden you are running late to pick up your child. When you first start school, you will be asked to comprise a list of people who have the right to pick up your child in the event that you cannot. Periodically, make sure that this emergency contact list is up to date. Then, if something should happen and you cannot pick up your child, you can call one of these people to ask if they can help you out. Then, call the school to let them know who from the list will be picking up your child. Remind that

> **"**
> *History will judge us by the difference we make in the every day lives of children."*
>
> **Nelson Mandela**

person to bring photo identification with them. The school is responsible for your child and will not release them to anyone without your verbal or written consent.

Real-life Example:

We remember one night, half an hour past closing time, and we had one little boy left. Calls to his mom and home were unanswered. No one on the emergency list responded either. Tick tock time was passing and out of desperation we contacted his dad who lived out of state during the week for his job. Being miles away, he was of no assistance and had no clue who else we could call. So, we were thinking we may have to follow school policy and bring him to the police station, but we were saving that as a last resort. An hour later the mother arrived after receiving a voicemail. Apparently her teenage daughter was responsible for pickup, but forgot. Mom had a special work project to attend to that day. Our advice: check-in with the person responsible for pick-up especially if they are not used to doing it.

#52 Breaking Up is Hard To Do

Key Point:

Tell the teacher or Director if you and your spouse are separating. Also, let the teachers know if there is a custody battle or a restraining order against one of the parents or against any other individual involved in the child's life (i.e. friend, grandparent).

Summary:

O.K. so we totally understand that you don't want the world to know when you are going through a personal crisis. We've all been there at some point in our lives. However, when something big like a separation or divorce is going on it will most likely affect your child's behavior.

We have seen children act withdrawn, become nervous, more aggressive, or angry.

Why this is Important:

The teacher's don't mean to pry, but if you and your partner are separating, the teachers do need to know. First and

up, our main goal is for the welfare of your child. We want to make sure that your child's well being is our top priority, whether that means being there for your child or making sure that only certain people can pick up your child, but we can't do our job if we're not informed. If the break up is new and hard for you to discuss with everyone, just talk to the Director alone. The Director will then pass this information on to the staff and explain that it's still hard for you to talk about it right now; but by doing this you have alerted the school to the family changes and made your child our top priority.

Real-life Example:

As an example, we had a child who was always such an outgoing and happy little girl. Suddenly, she became withdrawn and somber. We mentioned this sudden change in behavior to mom a few times before she took us aside to admit that she and her husband had separated and he had moved out. Right after that, we had to call security as we noticed a couple standing some distance from the playground one day taking pictures. It turns out that it was this same child's grandparents (from the father's side) and they were broken-hearted because they were asked not to visit their granddaughter. Yes, these are things we need to be aware of for everyone's sake.

foremost, they want to be able to support and reassure your child that it was not anything they did to cause the separation. Secondly, the director and the teachers need to know if there is a custody battle or a restraining order against one of the parents or against any other individual involved in the child's life (i.e. friend, grandparent, uncle). If there is, the custodial parent needs to also re-examine the "emergency pick-up list", to ensure that only the individuals that are still on that list still have the right to pick your child up in case of an emergency or when you can't. Then, once the changes are made, the school will ensure that all the staff members know of the changes you have made. Although it is sad when families break

#53 Sneaking Out?

Key Point:

Let us know if your child will be leaving early for the day. We should be aware of any changes in their schedule for planning purposes as well as for security reasons. We don't want staff to panic because they are unaware of a schedule change.

Summary:

If you are planning to pick your child up early, be sure to let the teachers know. It's especially important to inform them if someone else will be coming to get your child. Even if that person is on an approved list of people who have permission to pick up your child, it's best to reaffirm this. You just hear so many stories these days of people "going off the deep end" that it's best to be safe than sorry.

Why this is Important:

Changes happen all the time in the children's schedule. Everything is much easier for everyone if the staff know in advance. Teachers can help by getting your child ready for your arrival. For example, if you would like to pick up your child during naptime, the teacher will make sure your child gathers their belongings before you arrive to prevent a disruption for those children that are resting. There have been times when a parent has scheduled a dance or martial arts class for their child and we'd find out from the child throughout the day. However if the staff knew ahead of time about the class, they could help the parent out by helping their child get ready for the class (putting on their leotard/dance outfit or martial arts gear). This way, the child is ready to go in case you get stuck in traffic or are running late.

Real-life Example:

We had a case where the parents had a bitter divorce and we had to know exactly who would be doing the picking up every day. There was one instance when the dad came unexpectedly and wanted to take his son home, but since he was not on the schedule that day we had to alert the mom. Ugh, what an ugly mess! So, just remember that since we are responsible for your child, help us do our job and make us aware of any schedule changes. This is important for both planning and security reasons.

ARRIVAL

STORY TIME

It was outside play time when an older couple was spotted across the street from the playground shooting pictures. Well, we figured it wasn't the Paparazzi and naturally began to think of more deviant scenarios. When approached, the two identified themselves as the grandparents of one of the children in our facility. They were taking pictures for their son (the dad) because he was temporarily restricted from seeing his daughter for a while because of divorce proceedings!

Unfortunately, we had no knowledge of the situation and definitely should have been informed. The mom later explained that she told the child she could discuss it with us if she wanted to. Probably not the best way to handle it, you think?

You don't have to share the intimate details and we understand it may be difficult to talk about, but the reality is there could have been an unfortunate outcome as the result of not sharing such important information.

#54 Don't Wind 'em Up!

Key Point:

Coming in and reading a story or participating in an activity is always welcome. However, when it turns to horseplay and children become over stimulated, it becomes chaotic. When you leave, it's the teacher's job to try to return the classroom to some normalcy.

Summary:

Parents are always welcome to come in and share in an activity with their child or the whole class. However, when it all just turns into horseplay and gets the kids over stimulated, it just causes chaos. Yes, we have had parents who have done just that! When other children see this type of play, they often want to join in, which can turn into bedlam. When you leave, it's the teacher's jobs to return the classroom to normalcy, and if the teacher is alone with 10 children it can be a daunting task.

Why this is Important:

When you come in to drop your child off in the morning, it is always appreciated when you take some time to settle your child in before you leave for work. The same is true for the end of the day as well, when you come to pick them up; it's important for you to engage your child and show them that you missed them and ask about their day. By simply helping them to join and participate in an activity, you've also helped your child transition into the routine of the day. However, if your child gets excited while you are there, please find a way to calm them down. Suggest to your child that they find a book for you to read; this will calm their bodies down and give you bonding time together.

Real-life Example:

One of our recollections is of a dad who would bring his child in at circle-time and would interrupt by yelling hello and start encouraging the kids to get up and piggy pile on top of him! Once they were all out of control he would just get up and leave. Do you think the teachers had a happy face? Uh, no! There we were left with the task of calming them all down again. We weren't sure why he got such a kick out of doing this. Whatever the reason, we did have to have a little chat with him about it. Did he listen? Not really. If you would seriously like to spend some time in your child's classroom, make plans in advance to read a book or lead an activity. Or why not just join in what we are doing? That's great! But please don't just wind them all up!

ARRIVAL

69

Key Point:

Let the teachers know how your child slept the night before. Lack of sleep affects your child's temperament. Was your child awakened by a storm or a bad dream? Having this information can help us better manage your child's day.

Summary:

Most infant and toddler rooms have sign in sheets where you may share information about your little one. This is where you can relay any important happenings like how they slept the night before. It really is a good idea to inform the teachers of a rough night. Whether it was from a nightmare, a storm, or just not feeling well, lack of sleep affects your child's temperament just like it does yours!

Why this is Important:

When a child doesn't sleep the night before, it can affect their whole day. They can become easily upset and tearful, angry or just disgruntled about anything they are asked to do. If your child had a difficult time sleeping the night before due to a storm or were woken up in the night because of bad dreams, please take the time in the morning to give the teachers a heads-up. This way they will be aware of any unusual behavior or character changes in your child. As children age, they become more cognitive and they have a greater imagination, which at times can create nightmares. Some people believe that children only have nightmares due to cartoons or characters portrayed as bad guys on their TV shows, but that's not always the case. Sometimes children overhear the news or events that are happening around them and they get scared, if they don't voice these fears, their fears can show up in their dreams.

Real-life Example:

One four year-old boy, almost overnight, started to have a fascination with Spiderman. For this little boy, this was out of character for him. He had three older brothers that he liked to mimic. They loved sports and they played hard. Like his brothers, this little guy usually played rough and hard and had the same fascination for sports. Suddenly, he stopped playing games and started playing Spiderman. Then, he began to have nightmares during rest time. When the dad came to pick his son up, we told him he had a nightmare at nap-time and asked if he was having them at night too. He didn't think he had, but said he would keep an eye on him. The next day his dad informed us that his son had a difficult time sleeping the night before, due to nightmares, but he said his son wouldn't talk about the dream. When it came to nap-time, we thought this little boy would sleep well because he looked so tired, but once again he had awoken from a nightmare. The teacher brought him out of the classroom, into the light to

WE RECOMMEND:

Miss Nelson is Missing!
By Harry Allard and James Marshall
Publisher: Sandpiper Press

comfort him. After he was calmed down, she got him talking about what was scaring him so much. During the conversation, he asked the teacher, "How will daddy get me back if someone takes me?" While trying to reassure the boy that he was safe, the teacher got him to tell her more. She learned that his brothers were talking about some of the recent abductions in the area that were broadcast on all the local news channels. This little boy's brothers were in grade school and they were talking with their friends, and then one of the brother's asked this little boy, what he would do if someone took him. That question plagued him and it was in his every thought and began to show in his behavior and in night terrors. When the dad came to pick his child up, we explained what his son had told us. He said, he always put the news on while dinner was being made. He never realized that his children were even listening to it.

#56 Ring-a-Ding Ding!

Key Point:

Please call if your child will be arriving late or will be absent.

Summary:

Please let us know if your child will be absent or arriving late. We are expecting your child and if he or she doesn't arrive, we have to assume something is wrong.

Why this is Important:

If the teachers know in advance that you are running late, one of them will be happy to help you transition your child into play, circle time or whatever activity is going on in the classroom.

If the class is outside when you drop your child off, please make certain that a staff member knows you have arrived. By hollering out, "Good Morning" or giving them a simple wave, you are letting them know your child is there. Since the staff's focus is on the children and their safety, please make sure that the teachers have acknowledged your arrival by nodding their head or returning your wave.

Real-life Example:

We heard about a situation where a mom had to bring her baby to daycare one morning, a task the dad typically had so this was out of the norm for her. Well, she totally forgot and drove straight to work leaving her infant in the backseat. A few hours later a co-worker discovered the lifeless body of the baby in the overheated vehicle. We can't even begin to imagine the incredible guilt that mom has to live with. Maybe this tragedy could have been avoided if the daycare had called questioning the absence. The bottom line is that it is up to you to notify the staff of any changes in your schedule.

? : **DAYCARE Did You Know**
In 2006, 56% of mothers with children under the age of 3 were employed, as compared to 34% in 1975. (Source: Zero To Three Policy Center)

#57 A Little Piece of Home

Key Point:

Separation anxiety is real. One thing we found helpful for a child having difficulty separating is having a picture of mommy, daddy, a sibling or a pet hanging in their cubby. Also, a piece of clothing with your scent, a security blanket, or a stuffed animal can work wonders.

Summary:

Separation anxiety can be a very serious issue for a young child and is perfectly understandable. Some children are just very attached to their parents and the initial childcare experience can be very stressful. This is also hard on the parents who must leave the child as well as the teacher who is left to try and give comfort.

Why this is Important:

As children age these feelings of separation anxiety go away, because they understand that their parents will be back to get them. Yet for the very young, they haven't learned this yet, so they will cry, scream and latch on to their parents, hoping they won't leave them behind. Having plenty of experience with this, we'd like to share some things we have found helpful in this situation. You could try hanging a picture of your family or special pet in their cubby. We had a little girl who would carry the photo around with her for about 15 minutes before she would settle in and begin her day.

Also, a piece of clothing with mom or dad's scent on it can ease the tension. Other objects of comfort from home can include a security blanket, or stuffed animal. Now some may discount these ideas and say that the child will just have to get used to it. That mentality is just a bit too harsh and in our eyes not developmentally appropriate. Our job is to make the child's experience as positive as it can be. They eventually give up these things as they begin to feel more at ease.

Real-life Example:

We had one child that carried around one of his mother's shirts every day for security. He started this practice at home. Whenever his mom and dad would go out for the evening, leaving him with a babysitter, he would walk around with one of his mom's shirts. When he began school, he continued this practice of carrying around one of his mom's shirts. That way he could always have her scent with him. Eventually, as he became more and more secure in his environment, the boy gave up the shirt.

#58 Leave 'em Happy!

Key Point:

Always leave your child with a positive statement. It's important to always leave your child with a positive statement they can carry with them for the rest of the day.

Summary:

We know, some mornings can be very trying and children can wear your patience down. So, go ahead and take a deep breath (yes this really does help) and leave by saying something like, "have fun today!" or "love you, and see you later." It's kind of nice if you even know what activity they will be involved in that day and you specifically tell them to enjoy that.

Why this is Important:

There have been times when a parent has come into the classroom clearly distraught and then would blurt out in frustration, "It's been a crazy morning in our house!" Whatever happened or whatever words were exchanged, remember it is best to break the negativity before you get to the school. Otherwise, whatever last words you exchange will resonate for a while and affect your child's morning.

Before you leave try to talk to your child about what had happened, so you can resolve hurt or angry feelings and make sure your child feels loved. Otherwise, their bottled up feelings may create problems for those around them. Your child may take their feelings out on others by hitting or pushing. They may also just begin to cry without any clear reason. If talking about the event makes it worse, find something else to talk to your child about to get them excited about their day. If you see a smile on your child's face, it's a sure sign that their mood is changing and you can feel confident heading out the door that your child's day will be better.

Real-life Example:

We had a parent who would always leave her little girl off with a negative remark and create bad feelings. It just totally set the child's day off on the wrong foot and sometimes became a self-fulfilling prophecy. The child felt like they could do nothing right, so why bother even trying. Just think about how you would feel if your spouse or your boss started off your morning with a negative statement. The day is over before it even begins. Yes, words matter.

LOVE YA!

#59 Make a Clean Get-Away!

Key Point:

Some parents have a difficult time leaving their children at daycare. Do not keep saying goodbye and lingering. Get your child settled, say goodbye, and depart even if he or she is crying. We can tell you from experience the crying stops quickly.

Summary:

Some parents truly have a difficult time leaving their children off at childcare. It's totally understandable. Some of us can't even leave our cat at the vet without getting emotional! Ha! The thing is, you have made the decision to do this, so let's make this a good experience from beginning to end. It's so important that you say goodbye, when you are ready to leave, and then go. Do not linger! This sends mixed messages to your child.

Why this is Important:

A child can interpret a parent's outward feeling of separation as doubt. The child that is already feeling their parent's uncertainty begins to get more upset and clingy. You want to create certainty and comfort for your child. You can accomplish this by behaving confidently, even if it is difficult to do, in how you act and in what you say.

Real-life Example:

We have actually had moms admit that they feel like their children don't care about them if they don't break into tears when they leave.

In a weird way, we get it! But remember, you need to be the adult here. We remember one mom telling us she would go out to her car and cry almost every day for the first month. These feelings are normal. Feel free to call the daycare for some quick words of reassurance once you arrive at work. We don't want this to be a negative experience for you!

What Are We Doing Today?

Children get excited about learning and exploring new things. That's what makes teaching so worthwhile. In this chapter you will find ways in which you can enhance learning and creative experiences for your child.

A Note on Curriculum

Every center has a philosophy. Check this out carefully before you enroll your child. Ask what kinds of activities are involved in a typical day. It's important to be in a program with a curriculum you feel comfortable with. Being in a creative, nurturing, child-oriented and stimulating environment with age-appropriate activities will naturally foster the skills your child will need for success in his or her educational future. Remember, you literally have to learn to crawl before you learn to walk. People sometimes forget that children are constantly learning through all they do. A one-year old is mastering walking and talking and does not need to be on a computer, while a two-year old is trying to nail down that toilet training and does not need to worry about how to read.

#60 No Designer Duds!

Key Point:

Dress your child in clothes that they can get messy in. Children at this age are learning to do things for themselves and are using materials designed to build their finger strength. Spills and accidents will happen.

STORY TIME

A beautiful little girl arrived at preschool for her first day. She was immaculately dressed. Upon walking in the door she immediately took her shoes off. She would play with dolls, games, color and look at books. However, when something "messy" came out, such as paint, water table, or clay, she would back away. And while friends would encourage her to join in, she would not go near the sandbox! The reason for her behavior became evident one day when she finally, gleefully jumped into that sandbox and had a blast. When dad arrived at the end of the day he was annoyed at all the sand in her shoes and concerned about getting sand and dirt in his car.

He requested that she never go near the sand again – a request, by the way, that fell on deaf ears. Maybe dad should have built more mud-pies when he was a child! Exploring different materials is an important part of childhood. Please don't deny them the fun.

Summary:

The chances of keeping clothes clean are pretty slim. Children are in daycare on average about eight hours. During this time they are engaged in project activities, outside time, and eating.

Why this is Important:

During the preschool years, teachers offer children many different art mediums like finger paint, cornstarch and water, glues and pastes, and painting with various items such as: brushes, rollers or even household kitchen gadgets and sponges. They do this for many reasons. First, most children gravitate to the art materials. The colors and textures give children the opportunity to explore their senses. Secondly, these activities strengthen their fine motor skills. By strengthening these skills, they will be able to improve their cutting, writing and become more self-sufficient which will prepare them for kindergarten. Along with giving the children a variety of art materials to explore, the teachers also begin to let the children problem solve and use their fine motor skills to open up their own lunch items (yogurt, applesauce, fruit cups, puddings and juice boxes). This is another way to build those important fine motor skills; however, before they can successfully open their lunch items, many spills and accidents will happen. Don't make your child feel guilty about having dirt or stains on their clothes. This can lead to inhibited behavior.

Real-life Example:

There was a child in our care several years ago who actually became hesitant to play and once we got to the bottom of it she told us that she didn't want to do things because she might get dirty and her father would be angry. Wow! How sad is that? Once we told the parents that it was affecting her day, they stopped and that little girl was literally transformed into a new little person who just loved coming to school to participate in all that was offered! So please, leave the designer clothes at home for those special occasions.

> **"**
> *Children are likely to live up to what you believe of them."*
>
> Lady Bird Johnson

#61 Beautiful Junk

Key Point:

Things that you consider trash are treasures to your child's school.

Summary:

There are many things that your child's school would love to have around for the child's creative art experiences. Hopefully the program you send your child to is a creative one and would appreciate things like empty paper towel or toilet tissue rolls, old greeting cards, ribbons, egg cartons, oatmeal containers, empty boxes - all these objects can be used to create awesome art projects!

Why this is Important:

One of the school's goals should be to foster children's creativity. While playing, children use their imagination in different ways. It is mostly observed in their play. They may line up the chairs to create a car for everyone to sit in or use a cylinder shaped block as a fire hose while pretending to be a fire fighter. However, when the children play during the day, they are usually playing in small groups of children. So their ideas are a group effort. Therefore, the best way for the children to shine and show off their individual creativity is when they are offered "Open Ended" art. Open Ended art means there is no set goal or set outcome and the material used is of the children's choosing. By offering the children an array of various material and objects, it can expand their imagination and creativity. We're here to tell you that what you consider trash is truly treasure and that your child's classroom would love to have them. Something as simple as the screw top on your milk containers would make a great control panel for their rocket ship.

Here is list of some of the items that parents have brought into the classroom over the years:

- Scraps of fabrics
- Scraps of wrapping paper
- Paper towel or toilet paper tubes
- Cardboard squares
- Egg cartons
- Cotton balls
- Q-tips

- Buttons
- Yarn
- Ribbon
- Old/Used Holiday cards
- End of the roll Newspaper Print
- Small shoeboxes
- Film canisters
- Contact paper
- Small wood pieces
- Beans of different colors
- Seamstress scraps
- Toothpicks
- Popsicle Sticks
- Beads of all colors

Real-life Example:

When we worked for a hospital daycare, the parents kept us supplied with colored button caps from med bottles and we used those for all kinds of things! It is wonderful to see children create their masterpieces from recycled objects. Small containers, like yogurt cups can also be used to put paint and other art supplies in. All you need is some imagination and you can put most things to good use!

DAYCARE Did You Know

In 2007, there were over 740,000 childcare facilities in the United States, nearly four times the number than were in existence 20 years earlier. (Source: U.S. Census Bureau)

#62 To Each His Own

Key Point:

Not every child will participate in every project. They all have their own interests. Don't be alarmed if they haven't joined in an activity.

Summary:

Keep in mind that children develop likes and dislikes just like adults do and are attracted to certain activities and others not so much. Parents can become overly concerned if their child doesn't embrace all the activities that are offered. Our response to that is "relax!" Different strokes for different folks as they say. Your child will gravitate naturally to one activity more than another and may even refuse to do something.

Why this is Important:

Over the years there have been times when parents have expressed concern when their child wasn't bringing home art activities or showed any interest in an up and coming activity that the class was going to do. This is perfectly normal. Even at a very young age,

children begin to have interests and show their preferences in their play or the activities that they choose. Children will always gravitate to what interests them and ask to do that activity over and over again. If a child has a creative personality, they are most likely drawn to activities that allow them to express this part of themselves. If the child is a logical thinker, they are always trying to figure out or solve a problem in their play.

Real-life Example:

As an example, it's not uncommon to come across a child who does not want to participate in music time. There is nothing wrong with him or her sitting and observing. Forcing a child to participate just makes things worse. From experience we know that children come around in their own time.

#63 Parent Show & Tell

Key Point:

When you have a chance, share a little time with us. Come on in and read the kids a book or share some knowledge. One dad came in to tell us all about Hanukkah; he came prepared with props. The kids loved it.

Summary:

If you have the chance and ambition, why not share a little time with your child's class! Come on in and read a treasured book, teach us a favorite craft, show off a special or unique talent or share a family tradition. When you think about it, everyone has something to share if they want to. Think about it and set up a day to come in!

Why this is Important:

Whenever we ask the children what they enjoy doing the most with their mom or dad, they are always quick to respond. Your child is proud of you and loves doing things with you. Parents have taken time out of their day to come into their child's classroom to do something with the class. Whether that is to teach everyone about a family tradition, cook something, do a project with the kids, or just read a book. Their child showed great pride and excitement that their mom or dad were there and talked about it all day. If you have an idea of something you may want to do with your child's class just let them know. Your child will feel so special that you are there. Don't wait until your child goes into the elementary schools to show your interest and support. This is your child's first school experience; make it special by doing something within their class.

Real-life Example:

Here are a few examples:

- A mom came in and read stories about Alaska, right after their family came back from visiting there.

- A father came in to play his guitar, while

singing some of his daughter's favorite tunes.

- A parent, who was a chef, came into the classroom with a tray of cookies and everything the children needed to decorate them.

- We had a mother who came in to read stories and sing songs and then sat to have snack with the class.

- Another mom who came in with supplies to do a science experiment with the class.

- A mom who loved gardening decided to plant some flowers into large pots with the children to beautify the landscape.

- We had a parent bring in their new family puppy. They brought it in every month for that year, so the children could see how much it grew.

#64 Plant that Seed!

Key Point:

Children and teachers love gardening projects. Unfortunately, they can be costly. If considering a gift for the school, potting soil and seeds are always a good idea.

Summary:

Children just love to plant! How they love to get their hands in the soil and dig. And once they plant a seed they can't wait to watch it grow; it gives them such a sense of accomplishment. So if you are considering donating any materials to your child's classroom, potting soil, seeds, and containers are always welcome. Beans are great because they grow quickly and we

can add to the experience by reading Jack and the Beanstalk. Oh, how the imaginations run wild!

Why this is Important:

Teachers would love to do more special projects with children, but usually the cost is what stops them. Preschools don't make a lot of money and are on a tight budget. Teachers look forward to projects such as gardening, because it's a project that the children can work on one day and nurture it by watering it throughout the following weeks. Then as the plant grows, the children experience the science in the growing process. Then, later on when the plant gets big enough the children will learn new words by identifying the parts of the plant (roots, stem, leaf, petals and stigma). Finally, the teachers know that their investment will be enough to cover its cost, since it only requires a large bag of potting soil, some seeds and small flowerpots for each child.

Real-life Example:

We have had parents do a successful project at home with their child and want to share the idea with the school. This is great, but remember that many schools might not be able to afford to purchase the necessary supplies. If you have an idea, please consider the cost prior to making any promises. Of course if you want to purchase the materials, I'm sure every teacher would be thrilled!

#65 Venture Out!

Key Point:

If there is an activity your child enjoys doing at home, please feel free to pass the idea on to the teachers. We're always looking for new ventures.

Summary:

Do you have an activity that your child enjoys participating in at home that you would be willing to share with the class? Then please feel free to do so! Some parents have even been willing to come in and share their activities. Whether it is reading a special book, doing a project, or entertaining with a special talent, it is welcome. What a nice change of pace for the children as well as the teachers. That's what it is all about, sharing and learning from one another!

Why this is Important:

Children love it when a parent or even a relative come in for a visit and lead the activity for the day. Over the years, some great ideas have been passed down from the parents themselves. So, if you do an activity with your child at home, or you happen upon an idea in a magazine, from a friend or just on your own, please share it with staff. It may be something that they'd like to do with the whole class.

Real-life Example:

We have had individuals who have come in to play musical instruments, cook with the children, read a story, make a craft, and plant a garden. One dad

even came by to show the class how to ride a unicycle. Another parent found a book with science projects in it. The book offered science projects that were simple and intended to get young children interested in science at an early age. After seeing the book, the teachers went out and got their own copy and had many fun science projects with the class.

#66 All Dressed Up!

Key Point:

Preschool children love to play dress-up. Dress-up clothes donations are always appreciated especially men's clothes.

Summary:

Ever watch your little one trying on your shoes or wearing an article of your clothing? It's sure to bring a smile to your face as they are having so much fun pretending to be "big." The dress-up corner is probably one of the most popular areas in a preschool classroom. We always try to keep it filled with as many props as possible. So, if you have any clothes you can donate, they are usually well received.

Why this is Important:

Toddlers and preschoolers love to play dress-up. For the very young child, their world is centered on their mom, dad, siblings and grandparents. So their role-play is often something very simple. They choose nurturing roles or situations that are familiar to them in their everyday life. As children get a little older and their world expands, they begin to notice more people around them and the people that cross into their lives, and then they begin to include them into their role-playing situations.

Real-life Example:

We always asked for men's clothing, particularly things like sport jackets, ties, and vests. People tend to forget that boys play dress up too! And you are sure to be a big hit if you can find old dance recital costumes to bring in! Dramatic play is such an important part of a child's development as they are exploring their world and trying to make sense of it all. We can remember getting such a laugh out of two little girls who were playing "school" one day and how we overheard them saying "oh is there a full moon, these kids are wild today!" Something we had said earlier that morning. Too funny!

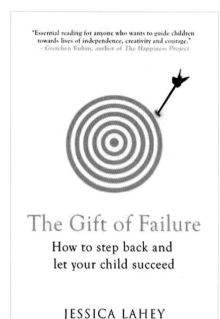

WE RECOMMEND:

"Essential reading for anyone who wants to guide children towards lives of independence, creativity and courage."
- Gretchen Rubin, author of *The Happiness Project*

The Gift of Failure

How to step back and let your child succeed

JESSICA LAHEY

The Gift of Failure: How to Step Back and Let Your Child Succeed
by Jessica Lahey
Publisher: Short Books, Ltd

#67 More Than Just Child's Play

Key Point:

Preschool children should play. It is developmentally appropriate and how they learn. Developing socialization skills, self-control, self-confidence, manners, and creativity - these are truly the basics needed to move on to the academic subjects. This concept is sadly getting lost today.

Summary:

We don't know exactly how or when it happened, but people started to think that preschoolers needed to be more academic. This line of thinking is so sad and so wrong. Play is the foundation of learning that leads to more complex thinking down the road. It also leads to happier and less stressed out children! You can't build a strong house without pouring the proper foundation first.

Why this is Important:

As children play within the classroom, here are examples of the extra benefits they are obtaining along the way. When playing with blocks: problem solving, hand-eye coordination, early math and science skills, and most importantly, learning to work together are all evident in their play. The younger children usually build with larger and heavier blocks, which aid in their physical development. Yet, as the children get older, they work together using the smaller block, which gives them practice with hand-eye coordination and most importantly they work in groups, which allow them to work on their social skills. Playing is often socialization (entering into the groups play, adjusting their own behavior to be part of the group, participating cooperatively, offering ideas, negotiating and accepting suggestions as well as taking turns). While building, they practice thinking out of the box and are using their imagination to create and recreate to construct buildings, cars, airplanes or anything else they can imagine. They begin to understand basic shapes, sizes and positioning of the blocks. They use math skills when they count how tall their building is, as well as adding and subtraction when they want to change something, telling their friends to put on three more or to take off two to see what would happen. Role-playing is the best way to see how the child views their world. They often role-play the people that are in their immediate lives. As they get older, they explore other roles (kings, queens, princesses, astronauts, race car drivers, doctors...etc.) Through all this they are exploring emotional and social roles in life, building self-esteem as the child realizes he/she can be anything when pretending. Dramatic play can nurture their thinking; expanding

ACTIVITY

83

their language and cooperation skills while it helps them with problem solving. Music and movement develops cognitive and physical skills. Physical skills such as balance and coordination of their large muscles while performing movements like skipping, galloping, or walking on their tip-toes to name a few. They work on their cognitive skills through memorization or recalling words to songs and chants and also by following simple directions. They explore rhythm and tonal highs/lows and foster creativity when they make up words having similar sounds. Even though the teachers know that the children are learning through their play, they also guide their learning as well.

Real-life Example:

During one conversation, a woman started talking about her daycare and how upset she was when she went to pick up her little girl and "all" she was doing was dancing!" Comments like this just make us cringe! What exactly should a four year old be doing, studying for the SATs? Come on now! And by the way, while that child was "just dancing" she was using coordination skills, self-expression, and getting exercise. Play sets the foundation for learning academics and that needs to be understood!

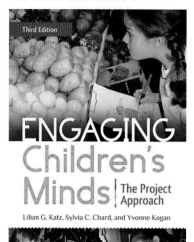
#68 Toys...Did You Say Toys?

Key Point:

If you wish to donate some of your child's old, but well cared for toys, check with your school's director or teacher first to make sure the toys are needed.

Summary:

From time to time a daycare will get a well-meaning soul who would like to donate all of their old and no longer used toys to the center. It is a nice gesture, but sometimes the donations may not be usable because of certain state mandated restrictions. For instance, some areas require that all sliding and climbing equipment be secured to the ground. However, books that are in good condition are usually welcome as schools can add them to their library area. Always check with the director before you begin hauling things in.

Why this is Important:

When parents find that their child is no longer playing with a particular toy, they often put it away. After a while, parents find themselves clearing away all the old toys to make room for new ones. If you are looking for a place to donate all of these toys, you might want to consider your child's school. Schools are on a tight budget and can't always buy toys as often as they'd like to or need to. With so many children using the school's toys, they get broken easily.

Real-life Example:

Many toys that may be perfectly fine for home use cannot be used in a school setting. Years ago we worked at a school that refused to allow used stuffed animals to be donated because of the difficulty getting them clean, the likelihood of germs, and the possibility of spreading lice.

#69 Scrap Booking 101

Key Point:

Children love to save their own artwork. However, this can become overwhelming. To keep memories and special projects without the clutter, take a picture of the work and start a scrapbook.

Summary:

It's so neat to watch children create and observe how their art work changes just within a year. They are so proud of their creations and you just wish you could keep it all. When children first have to make the decision of what to throw away, it can be very hard for them. However, to make this task easier and to keep the memories of their drawings and special projects without the clutter, take a picture of their work and start a scrapbook for them.

Why this is Important:

As children get interested in drawing and using all the art materials available to them, everything they make becomes very important to them. Without a doubt, it is hard to keep everything your child makes, but you have to let them have an active role in deciding what they want to keep, as well as what they want to throw away. We have had some parents purchase an art portfolio for their child to put all of their creations in, and then when the portfolio gets too full it will be the child's job to decide what is important to them and want to keep, and what can be thrown away.

Real-life Example:

Of course there are the pages and pages of "scribbles" that as one parent put it, "have to discreetly go into the ol' circular file." It was this same parent who said that what she does is keep some artwork and the others she will take pictures of and store in a scrapbook. What a great idea! It keeps those special projects without taking up so much room.

ACTIVITY

#70 Nothin'

Key Point:

Don't be surprised or concerned if when asked what they did at school your child responds with, "nothing". Ha! They will come out with little "tidbits" of information when they feel like it. You may even hear a new song or story while they're playing at home.

Summary:

Just sit back for a minute and think about your childhood. How many times did you reply with "uh nothing" or "just stuff" whenever your parents asked what you did at school that day? Ha! Are we right? Unless it was some major happening like someone getting into a fistfight and causing bleeding you were pretty much just going on with your routine. Well, not much has changed since then so don't be concerned if you ask your child what they did at daycare and they reply with "nuttin!" and a shoulder shrug. They will eventually come out with little tidbits when they feel like it. You may even figure out what was happening or hear a new song or story as they are playing by themselves.

Why this is Important:

Often parents get distressed when they ask their child, "What did you do today at school?" Often their child will respond, "I don't know", or "Nothing".

NOTHIN'

You may think it's a simple question, "What did you do all day?" But truly, it's not! The question is too broad, too general.

Sometimes when something happens throughout the day that upsets your child or makes them extremely happy, this stays in their memory and they will recall it easier. For instance, your child had a fight with a peer in the class. Or, your child waited all morning to use a particular toy and then it was clean up time and they never got to use it. They may remember a special event that took place at school, such as, the school had a lady come with snakes! She was holding a really, really long snake that wrapped all over her body! Events like these help your child remember things that happened within the day, because they have an emotional connection to the event. Therefore, don't be surprised if your child remembers instances within the day where they felt as if they were wronged or remembers something that really excited them; they will remember these things before they can tell you about their day as a whole or even one specific thing.

Real-life Example:

If you want to start a specific conversation with them take note of the activities they were involved in that day (they are usually listed on a board somewhere in the classroom). We used to write a quick and short note on something the child did that day and send it home. Or simply take out a project the child brought home and ask questions about it. That might be a conversation starter, but again don't worry if it is not.

? : **DAYCARE Did You Know**
46 percent of daycare services are provided in stand-alone buildings. Churches and other places of worship account for 20 percent.
(Source: Department of Education; National Center for Education Statistics)

Yeah, Let's Get That Energy Out!

Getting outdoors to play is crucial to any childcare program. Movement and fresh air is certainly a stress relief for children and staff. The following information will make that time more enjoyable for your child.

#71 Boots or No, Out We Go!

Key Point:

Please assume your child will be going outside and provide appropriate clothing for outdoor play. Otherwise, staff is scrambling around to find spare clothes that don't always fit so well.

Summary:

Most daycare centers will have the children go outside on a daily basis. Both the children and the teachers need this time to just unwind after being cooped up inside together. Please remember to provide appropriate clothing for outdoor play. This is especially important in climates that experience cold and snowy winter days. We can't keep the whole class in because one child is unprepared.

Why this is Important:

There have been times when parents have forgotten some

or all of their child's outdoor gear. It's not the school's responsibility to supply your child with outdoor wear. For winter climates, some schools may have a small bin of donated snow gear: snow pants, boots and mittens. The teachers do their best to try to find something to keep unprepared children warm. Sometimes when the parents are called to bring in their children's snow gear, the parents will ask if their child can just stay inside. This is not an option. Schools do not have extra staff members to stay with the children who are not properly prepared to go outside. We know you have a lot to remember in the morning, but making sure your child is prepared for outside play is still your responsibility. If it's too much to bring it all in daily, then leave your child's snow gear in their cubby all week, bringing it home on the weekend to wash.

Real-life Example:

We had one little boy, without his own boots, who absolutely dug his heels in because he would not wear the pair of purple boots with flowers on them! Ha! It was all we could find! One of our coworkers, who always got annoyed when kids didn't have all the proper outerwear, would chant, "boots or no, out we go!"

#72 Go To Extremes

Key Point:

Unless the weather is extreme (freezing cold, high humidity and heat, etc.) the children should get outside on a daily basis. Question it if they don't. Physical exercise is important!

WE RECOMMEND:

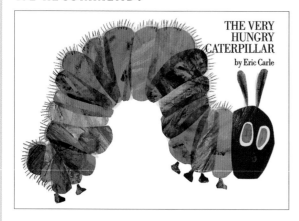

The Very Hungry Caterpillar
by Eric Carle
Publisher: Philomel Books

Summary:

Unless the weather is extreme (freezing cold, high humidity and heat, etc.), the children should get outside on a daily basis. Physical exercise and freedom to be loud is a very important part of their day. On the other hand, you may want to inquire on those extreme weather days if your child will be staying in. Being out in extreme heat or cold is not safe, but some teachers may want to venture out anyway because they just don't want to be cooped up all day. Ask what kind of physical activities they plan for indoors. There should be an area where they can put out equipment such as gym mats, indoor slides or climbers, and small riding toys. Find out what their rainy day back up plans are.

You should always plan ahead and bring your child's outdoor necessities in with the assumption that they "will" be going outside. This statement is true no matter the season or the weather. During the warmer weather you will need to provide your child with sneakers and sunscreen. Some schools even ask that you bring in a bathing suit and a towel for sprinkler play.

When the weather is cold, you will need to bring in a coat, hat and mittens. Then after a snowfall, you will also need to bring in boots and snow pants. If you live where there is snow, snow pants are a must. However, some places may not get snow, but it still gets cold. Snow pants are still useful because they add a layer of protection for your child while they play on the hard frozen ground. When the ground begins to thaw, it often becomes extremely muddy. By wearing snow pants, or a lighter weight version of these known as mud pants, the children's clothes are protected. Without this type of protection, your child ends up changing their clothes two to three times a day after playing outside. This causes an extra burden on you because you will have to keep bringing in extra spare clothes daily.

Outdoor play is so beneficial to the children; it expands on their gross motor skills (running with speed and control, using their upper body to pull themselves up, kicking balls with control and distance), while at the same time strengthening their foundation and increasing their balance.

Real-life Example:

One winter a mom questioned why we were not taking the kids out as often in the afternoon as we had done so previously. This mom was paying attention. Turns out we were down to one staff member in the afternoon and it was too chaotic for one teacher to get all the kids dressed up in winter gear all by herself. As self sufficient as the kids are, getting them ready to go out in the cold is not as simple as it sounds. We gave her credit for asking because she felt it important that her little guy get out in the fresh air and use up some of his high energy. Good for her!

#73 Some Sun Sense

Key Point:

During the summer, it would be helpful if you could apply sunscreen on your child before sending them to daycare or preschool.

Summary:

So the hot summer months are here and we need to chat a bit about sunscreen. First of all, it would be greatly appreciated If you could apply sunscreen on your child before you leave the house, then they will be all set for going out in the morning. If you supply sunscreen for the teachers and staff to apply to your child, a spray on type is much easier and quicker. Your child may be involved in some kind of water play so be sure it is the waterproof kind. Please note that most daycare centers now require you to sign a document giving permission to apply sunscreen to your child. This is in case there are any adverse reactions to the product.

Why this is Important:

First and foremost it would be extremely helpful if you would apply the first application of sunscreen onto your child just before you get them dressed in the morning. Can you imagine how difficult it is to properly apply it to a large group of children? By you applying it yourself, this will ensure that your child has the proper coverage and there will be no missed areas. Most preschool programs go out twice a day, in the morning and then again in the afternoon. The sun may not be as strong in the afternoon hours, but some children may need a second application of sunscreen because their skin is so fair or their parent would like to keep their child protected. If you would like to have the teachers reapply some on your child, just let them know. It is best to bring in a sunscreen that is water resistant and a spray-on. We like to get even the smallest of the daycare population out in the fresh air for a while whenever possible. So please remember

> **"**
> *Your child will see what you're all about by what you live rather than what you say."*
>
> Wayne Dyer

to send in a sun hat for those hot and sunny days when the babies may go out for a short stroll in the carriage. Babies six months or younger should not have sunscreen.

Real-life Example:

One boy, Gregory, had sunscreen applied to him by his dad just before being dropped off. The dad was a little rushed and did as good a job as he could applying the sunscreen. However, later in the day after Gregory had required a change of his shirt because of a spill, the teachers noticed a red blotch on his chest. It turns out when Gregory changed his shirt, the area underneath had not received sunblock earlier and was exposed all afternoon to the sun. To prevent this from happening, try to get the sunblock thoroughly applied before your child gets dressed.

#74 Name It To Claim It

Key Point:
Please take the time to write your child's name on the inside tags of their jackets, sweaters, snow pants, mittens, or hats.

Summary:

Ever try to get a roomful of 2-year olds ready for outdoors? Please be sure you have labeled all of your child's outdoor gear. This includes jackets, sweaters, boots, hats or mittens. It's best to use a permanent marker for this and write it on the inside tag of the items. If you want to put it directly on the material a metallic permanent marker will work.

Why this is Important:

When the children are very young the teachers assist them to dress for outdoor play. However, as the children get older, they are encouraged to attempt one task at a time on their own. This way, by the time they go off to kindergarten, they will be more self- sufficient. For that reason, by age 3, the children are cheered on as they practice and take small steps to complete one task at a time. However, it's common for several children to come into school with the same style coat and none of them have been labeled. If items are properly labeled, there will be no confusion around which child they belong to.

Real-life Example:

We can't tell you how many times when,

in the chaos of getting a group of young children ready to go out, things have become mixed up. We'll never forget a little girl going into a full tantrum for twenty minutes because we had put someone else's snow pants on her body! Ai yi yi! It's best to avoid these moments, don't you think?

#75 No Place Like Home

Key Point:

If you feel your child is too sick to participate in outdoor play, then they should be home where it's nice and cozy.

Summary:

Sometimes a parent will request that a child stay inside that day because they are feeling "under the weather." Well, we are here to tell you that will go over like a lead balloon! That request is easily translated to mean, "My kid is sick, but I brought him in anyway." If you feel that your child is too sick to do all of the activities that are offered, then they shouldn't be at school.

Why this is Important:

Outdoor play is part of the daily schedule.

It isn't practical in this environment to let one child remain inside while the entire class is outside. That scenario would require supervision in both places and centers aren't staffed for that. And the whole class isn't going to remain inside just because of one child feeling under the weather. The bottom line is, if the child is well enough to come to school, that means they are expected to participate in all of the things their classroom is doing, including going outside.

Every winter when it starts getting cold outside children start to show signs that something is brewing, like a runny nose, sneezing, or a low-grade fever. It never fails that we get a parent who will say something like this, "Bobby's nose is running today, is there any chance that he can stay inside when the others go out to play?" The simple answer to that question is no. The school simply does not have a spare individual who can do "one on one" with your child.

#76 Hand Me Downs

Key Point:

We understand that keeping up with all the outerwear kids need for snow can get costly – they grow so quickly! Suggest that your facility provide a box for hand-me-downs from other parents. This idea is usually well received.

Summary:

Children grow quickly! You don't want to be caught off-guard when the colder weather arrives. If you work with the school to establish a hand-me-down box, it will benefit many children and parents for years to come.

Why this is Important:

Each year we have the same concern: parents who are unprepared for their child's outdoor winter gear. Gloves are the first thing overlooked. When the temperature drops, the children have nothing to protect their hands during outdoor play. This can be painful when their fingers touch the cold medal on the swings, bikes or other equipment. Parents scramble and pull out last year's snow gear, only to learn that it is much too small.

Real-life Example:

We've suggested to parents that they browse the local consignment shops for winter outerwear. Sometimes, if a bargain is available, a few parents will purchase multiple items and donate them to the hand-me-down box for others to use. We could all appreciate saving a little money, especially for something that has such a limited wearing time.

#77 Ouch!

Key Point:

Provide a pair of sneakers for your child to wear during outside time. Most playgrounds have an absorbent material, such as woodchips, to protect the children from falls. However, these materials can be painful if your child is wearing sandals or flip-flops.

Summary:

Yes, we get it. There are some very cute and stylish footwear out there these days for the little ones and you just can't resist. However, while they may look fashionable and cool, the thing is they are really not appropriate for outside play, especially when the little darlings are climbing around on the playground equipment.

Why this is Important:

If your child insists on wearing the more trendy shoes to school, then make sure you have also sent along a pair of closed toe shoes or how about just a good old pair of sneakers so that your child's outdoor experience remains a fun and safe one. Whether your child wears sneakers to school, or if you just keep a pair in your child's cubby, sneakers are essential footwear for outdoor play. Playgrounds are designed with the children's safety in mind. Dirt and grass may seem like it will be enough to aid a child when they fall, but it really is not. Its ability to prevent injuries is greatly changed by the weather conditions. Cold weather makes the ground very hard and unyielding; rain causes dirt and grass

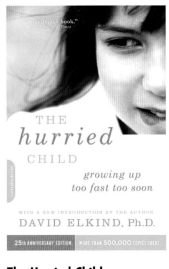

WE RECOMMEND:

THE *hurried* CHILD

growing up too fast too soon

WITH A NEW INTRODUCTION BY THE AUTHOR
DAVID ELKIND, Ph.D.

25th ANNIVERSARY EDITION   MORE THAN 500,000 COPIES SOLD

The Hurried Child
by David Elkind
Publisher: Da Capo Press

to become slippery. Therefore, each school is responsible for laying down protective ground cover. When children have improper footwear, such as sandals or flip-flops, it causes different safety issues. When children are running about, materials get stuck between their foot and their shoe and it can be quite painful. During the preschool years, children have many falls, because they have not yet learned how to run or easily change directions. As time goes on, they will obtain the ability to run with speed and control, but until then, having the proper footwear on will prevent many playground accidents.

Real-life Example:

We are not exaggerating when we say that many serious injuries are the result of children wearing clogs, Crocs®, sandals, flip flops, and shoes with no traction. They play hard out there and need something stable on their feet. We can't tell you how many times we've seen a little one run and trip over their flip-flops and dive head first into an object. OUCH!

DAYCARE Did You Know

? :   Children who attend high-quality preschool enter kindergarten with better pre-reading skills, richer vocabularies, and stronger basic math skills than those who do not.
(Source: National Institute for Early Education Research)

Hey, What's to Eat?

Most states require a childcare facility to provide a daily nutritional snack. Some facilities may even ask parents to send in a treat on occasion. You know all too well how challenging it is to feed one child, now imagine settling a whole group down to eat. This chapter will give you ideas on what to pack in that lunch box and suggest ways to make snack time and lunch a less chaotic point in the day for everyone.

#78 Food For Thought

Key Point:

Bad eating habits start at a young age and they are hard to break, so start teaching your child good eating habits as they grow.

Summary:

Each parent has his/her own idea of how they want their child to eat and sometimes even in what order they get their food. If you are fully engaged in what your child is eating to ensure healthy growth, then you need to be aware of the lunchtime and snack time policies of the school. They differ from place to place.

Why this is Important:

Learn what the school's policies are and if you would like your wishes carried over while your child is at school, let the staff know. Your child is at the age where they need to be guided to make the healthier choices of what they should eat. You do this at home with them at every meal.

Of course, a brownie is going to look better to a three year old, compared to their sandwich, yogurt or fruit. You can monitor what's going on by seeing what remains in their lunchbox at the end of the day. Just giving you some "food for thought".

Real-life Example:

We spent many wonderful years working at a childcare facility that was part of a Children's Hospital. During this time we were fortunate to have so many great resources available to us and learned a great deal! So we would like to share some things with you concerning your child's eating habits since that is always a main subject in daycare.

One thing that has always stuck with

us: a respected nutritionist said there are no GOOD foods and BAD foods, rather, ALWAYS and SOMETIMES foods. We love it! There are very few among us who can sustain strict diets of fruits and veggies and don't want to indulge in some chips or cake too!

Right?

Just because a child won't eat something like carrots, for instance, doesn't mean you should never present them again. Put out a plate with what you are eating, and let the child find what he or she likes.

#79 Chef's Little Helper

Key Point:

Get your child involved in making their lunches with you. Give them healthy choices and make them an active part in preparation: your child will learn good nutrition and eat better since they were involved with the choices.

Summary:

As we all know, kids are just typically picky little eaters and it can be difficult to navigate through the path of figuring out what to serve for lunch. We have found that children are more likely to try something if they have had a hand in the preparation. So why not have your child assist you with preparing lunch once in a while? You can also find cookbooks for children that include some simple and tasty recipes that you can make together. It will also give ideas on how to make food more appealing such as using cookie cutters to make fun sandwich shapes. The extra effort can lead to better eating!

Why this is Important:

Each year we always hear the same concern from parents,

"How do I get my child to eat their lunch?" These same parents get more frustrated and eventually ask for suggestions. We always tell them the same thing. Stop choosing for them. Get your child involved in putting their lunch together with you. If they have a role in what goes in there, then they are more likely to eat it. By being an active participant, your child will learn good nutrition and will begin to eat better.

Real-life Example:

We had one picky eater in our class who was actually willing to give guacamole a try because he had such a good time mashing up those pretty green avocados! Of course he also enjoyed dipping a few tortilla chips in it, too.

STORY TIME

We had one parent that was distraught because every night when she went home to wash out her child's lunch containers, she found most of her child's lunch remained untouched. Often the child ate the dessert and then the yogurt. The mother became very concerned when she saw the same thing happening over and over again, so she questioned the teacher. The teacher told this mother she was only following the school's policy which allows the child choose what she eats on her own. Needless to say, this parent wasn't aware of this policy and simply stated, "My three year old isn't making those kinds of choices yet. Tomorrow, I will have a number on her containers, please give them to her in that order. Also, from now on, my daughter is only to eat her dessert during afternoon snack. I will let her know too, so she knows these are my wishes."

#80 Plastic Please

Key Point:

Please do not send beverages or food in glass containers. There are too many opportunities for it to break throughout the day.

Summary:

How easily little elbows bump and tip things over and CRASH, the next thing you know there is shattered glass all over the table or floor. Sending in food or other things in a non-glass microwave safe container is definitely the better option.

Why this is Important:

Children will sit together at one table to eat their lunch. The children spread out their lunches and open and close their lunch boxes as needed. It is not unusual for one of the children to knock something over while they are trying to maneuver in their small spaces. Accidents do happen, but it's more serious when one of the children has a glass juice bottle or food container made of glass. When these get knocked off the table or dropped while the children are trying to clean up their lunches, shards of glass go everywhere! It is very difficult to clean up the glass. So for everyone's safety, please do not send any type of glass in your child's lunch box. They are too young to have that responsibility and accidents do happen!

Real-life Example:

We have noticed recently that more people are sending their children's food in glass containers. Sure, we get that you are trying to be more environmentally aware and feel it is safer in the microwave. However, we still feel it is a safety issue in the classroom.

#81 Cut It Out!

Key Point:

Lunchtime will go along much better for your child and the teachers if you peel and cut your child's fruit or veggies and store them in a plastic baggie. This saves time and makes things run smoother for everyone.

Summary:

Ah, lunchtime with a bunch of pre-schoolers, the thing indigestion is made of! Ha! We try to do whatever we can to make this particular time of day go as smoothly as it can. One thing you can do to help is to peel and cut up your child's fruit or veggies. If you want your child to actually eat the lunch you've readied for them, please take the time to prepare it so it's easier for them to eat.

Why this is Important:

Lunchtime can be chaotic. As children get older they eat on their own and the teacher's job is to assist the children only when needed. When it comes to lunchtime, the teacher's main goal is to prepare the children for kindergarten, where they will be expected to be self-reliant. Preparing them to be more self sufficient at lunch time will be easier if their lunches are prepared with a little more care at home. You want to provide

STORY TIME

⭐ One day at lunchtime, Pedro, one of the little boys, announced that he had made his own lunch with his mom. He was so proud. The teacher said, "Let's see what you chose to pack." The little boy pointed to each item and started to tell the class what he had, "I have some strawberries and blueberries, a cheese stick, yogurt, rice and beans and goldfishes."

The teacher replied, "Wow, you made some excellent choices."

The teacher then asked the class, "How many of you take a vitamin every day?"

Most of the class raised their hands. The teacher explained that our bodies need vitamins to make our bodies grow and work properly and told them you can give your bodies lots of vitamins from the good food you eat.

Then she looked over at Pedro's lunch and said, "Everything you have in here is so good for you because it has vitamins and other things that will help your body." She pointed to his container of blueberries and strawberries and said, "These give you lots of energy, they keep you healthy and they are good for your hair and skin." Then, she pointed to his yogurt and his cheese stick. "These have calcium and protein. The calcium will help your bones and teeth to be strong and the protein will keep your tummy full longer so you won't get hungry."

Pedro then picked up his rice and beans and said, "What about these?"

The teacher said, "The rice will give you energy to run fast and the beans are good for your heart."

Other children started to point to things in their lunchbox and holler out.

The teacher went through each item telling the children something basic that they could remember about what the food did for their bodies. Then, near the end of lunchtime, one of the little girls held up a chocolate cupcake and said, "What does this do for my body?"

The teacher gave herself a minute to think. Then, the other teacher in the class who was sitting at the girls table said, "Well Heather, they call that a sometimes food. Do you know why?" The little girl shook her head no and asked why. The teacher said, "because things like cakes, cupcakes and candy do not really have anything in them to make us grow stronger or healthier, that's why they are called sometimes foods. We should only eat them sometimes, even though they taste good, they are not good for us."

After that day, each day at lunchtime the children would all inquire about something they were eating and wanted to know how it helped their bodies. A few of the parents even told us that their child was requesting different things in their lunchboxes that were good for them.

your child with a lunch that encourages them to eat while giving them a sense of self-reliance. One of the best things you can do for your child is cut up their fruits and vegetables, which will make it easier for them to handle. Grapes, for example, are one of the biggest choking hazards in young children. Sometimes children are very chatty when they are sitting near their friends at lunchtime. If they are talking while eating a grape, it can slip right into their windpipe, creating a choking hazard. Therefore, grapes should be cut into fourths for very young children and then into half as your child gets older, to prevent any dangers of choking. Some parents really encourage their child to eat more vegetables, which is a great lesson to start in their early lives. However, when you put the whole carrot in their lunch, it doesn't look appealing to them and they often won't eat it. However, if you cut up that carrot into little matchstick-like pieces or coins, and give them something to dip it into, like ranch dressing, they are more excited to eat it.

Real-life Example:

If we were paid for every time we had to peel a fruit, we would be millionaires! Ha! Our hands are still stinging from the grapefruits and oranges we had to peel over the years. It simply isn't a good idea. The teachers are trying to get a whole room full of kids to sit and eat lunch and any time spent on preparing food is time away from the kids.

#82 Don't Lose the Good Silver

Key Point:

Check with your daycare facility for their policy on eating utensils. Some centers don't supply them.

Summary:

If you must send in eating utensils for your child, please use plastic and be sure to label them with your child's name. Children don't always clean up properly after lunch, if things are labeled, teachers can return them to the proper owner.

Why this is Important:

When there are 12, 14, 16 or even 20 children to a classroom, they will use 2 to 3 spoons per child per day, to cover morning snack, lunch and afternoon snack. Most states have a policy that the plastic-ware cannot be reused due to health reasons unless it came directly from the child's own lunch box. Schools are always looking for ways to keeps their costs down, and one of those ways is to ask the parents take turns supplying the class with plastic-ware or to have them put eating utensils in their own child's lunch box. By the age of 2 ½ years old, children are being guided to clean up their own lunch mess, however, they can easily get distracted and accidentally throw away your good silverware.

Real-life Example:

We often recommend to the parents to take a trip to the party store and find fun colored eating utensils (pink, red, yellow, blue, purple and green). We ask the parent to do this for two reasons. First, when all the children come in with plain white plastic-ware they can easily get confused to which fork or spoon was theirs at the table. Often, there are at least four children sitting together at a small table to eat, when one child puts down their spoon, another child may

LUNCH/SNACK

pick it up and start to use it, thinking it was theirs. On the other hand, if you go to the party store and get plastic-ware in your child's favorite color, they will always know which utensil is theirs even after they have put it down.

#83 No Additives Please

Key Point:

Do not put medicine in your child's thermos, expecting your child to get a second dose of a needed antibiotic or other medication. Another child may accidentally drink from your child's drink and get medication not intended for him or her. This is a major liability for you and the school!

Summary:

Surprisingly, we have encountered parents who have actually added medication to their children's juice cups in order to get them another dose of an antibiotic. Now, this is an absolute No-No! What if another child was accidentally given the wrong cup and ended up ingesting the medication? Worse yet, can you imagine if it was something the child was allergic to? Don't make the mistake of risking everyone else's safety by putting medicine in your child's lunch containers. If your doctor feels your child needs medication and the school doesn't give it, arrange to make yourself available to give it to your child and don't try to sneak it into their drinks.

Why this is Important:

You learn that your child has an ear infection or some other illness that requires timely medication, such as an antibiotic. Or maybe your child had a low grade fever that morning and you gave him Tylenol®, but to keep the fever down, you'll need to give them another dose later in the day. You get discouraged because your daycare either doesn't give medication or won't

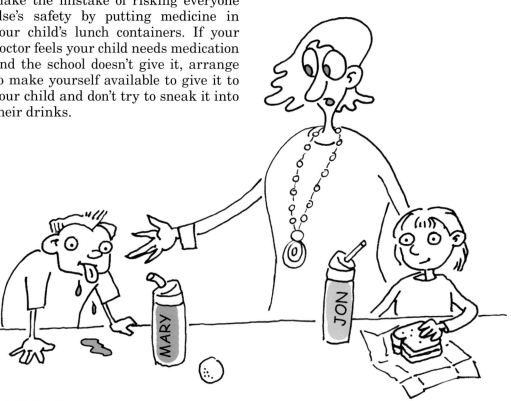

give something like Tylenol® without a doctor's written consent. That would mean that you would need to leave your job in order to give your child the medicine. Unfortunately, there have been times when a parent has just tried to sneak the medicine into their child's juice to save them a trip to the school, and they thought they'd drink it at lunchtime. This is very dangerous and can be a major liability for you and the school! During lunchtime, children are easily distracted. We can't even count how many times a child has sat down in another child's seat and started to eat or drink. So, if you put medicine into your child's drink container expecting your child to get their second dose at lunchtime and another child drinks it, the consequences can be serious, especially if the other child is allergic to the medication. Another scenario that happens often is your own child may take one sip of their drink and tell the teacher that their drink tastes funny and they didn't want to drink it. The teacher may assume that the juice had gone bad and poured it down the drain. Then, you will have no idea that your child isn't getting their needed medication.

Real-life Example:

We actually discovered that parents were adding medication to their child's drinks when several preschoolers said their juice "tasted funny." When questioned, the parents said they couldn't leave work to give their children the meds. Always make the teachers aware of any drugs your child may be on so they can react in case of an allergic reaction. And please make arrangements to have the medication dispensed to your child if absolutely necessary during the day. Sneaking it into a juice cup is not an option.

#84 Toothbrush Follies

Key Point:

It's not wise to have your child brush their teeth at school. The teachers cannot totally attend to this activity and left to doing this task alone, children get distracted and who knows where that toothbrush will end up! Yuck!

Summary:

Even though this is probably a mute point in most centers now, we're going to throw it out there anyway. It is not wise to have your child brush their teeth at school. One of the purposes of preschool is to build the children's attention span and help them to focus to complete a task on their own, by kindergarten. Until they learn to do this, children can get easily distracted. So expecting them to brush their teeth on their own is not wise and it can also be a health hazard.

Why this is Important:

After only a minute, the child who was left to brush his or her teeth can easily get distracted and instead of brushing their teeth they can be found brushing the sink with their tooth brush and then putting it back into their mouth! Children this age won't be able to complete this task without constant guidance, it's a given, and they shouldn't be expected to. Please keep the toothbrushes at home, where you can monitor your child and teach them the how to brush their teeth. It is not something that should be done at school.

Real-life Example:

At one daycare facility, all the children brought in toothbrushes and stored them in a container on the bathroom shelf. Talk about chaos! We would line up all the toothbrushes on the sink and slather toothpaste on them and, oh, let the games begin. There were children ending up with the wrong brushes, brushes being used to scrub the sink, swallowing of the toothpaste – you get the idea. It was soon decided that this routine should be eliminated. Of course if you are picking up your child to go to the dentist then by all means you can have them clean their teeth first under your supervision. Otherwise, leaving this particular routine to twice a day at home should be just fine.

#85 No Melt Downs

Key Point:

If your child's lunch is suppose to be heated, please send it in a microwave-able safe container. Also remember to label the container with your child's name.

Summary:

If you are sending in food that has to be heated, please make sure you are using a container that has the words, "Microwave Safe" on the bottom. Do not reuse containers that are intended to be recycled. These containers melt when they reach a certain temperature. Containers for margarine, yogurt, sour cream, deli or even take out containers from a restaurant are not microwave safe and may emit chemicals into your child's food.

Why this is Important:

Today, the Food and Drug Administration is regulating how plastic food containers are produced and many no longer contain chemicals in them. Still, you must remain vigilant. Choose your child's lunch containers carefully and be sure to look for the words, "Microwave Safe" on them. If you are concerned about chemical toxins leaking into your child's food when it's being heated, then send in a cold lunch for your child. Some parents purchase reusable sandwich bags. They are cloth on the outside and vinyl on the inside, and they close with a Velcro tab. They are easy to wash and quick to air-dry.

Real-life Example:

We can't tell you how many times we have destroyed containers in the microwave and in doing so had to find a substitute lunch for a child. Sorry about that one folks! So if your child's lunch needs to be heated, please send it in a microwaveable container. They are always clearly marked on the tags whether they are safe for microwaves, dishwashers, etc. And while we are talking about it, it would be helpful if you separated the foods to be warmed up from the ones that don't. In other words, if you don't want your child's grapes to be heated, please don't put them in the same dish as the chicken nuggets! Ha!

Key Point:

Don't be surprised if your facility asks parents to take turns and provide a healthy snack for the children one day a week. This is a common practice as facilities try to keep costs down.

Summary:

Children look forward to snack time. Hey, don't we all! Anyway, your center may ask you to sign up to provide a snack for the class or you may just opt to do so on your own. Please remember that your child gets excited about bringing in something special and may want to help you decide what to bring and even help make it. It is a good idea to try and come up with something healthy to share.

Why this is Important:

Schools ask families to take turns for two reasons. First, it is a way to keep costs down, and second, it provides a time for you to interact with your child in the kitchen. Please be sure to check with your teachers to see if any of the children in the class have a food allergy so you can plan accordingly. Also please remember that children under three should avoid small food items (choking hazards) as well as things that are too hard to chew. Bringing in colorful plates or napkins to serve your snack on is a big hit and makes anything taste good!

Keeping this in mind, we have a few suggestions listed below. These are just a few things we know children enjoy, but you may have your own specialty you want to share.

- Applesauce
- Cheese and crackers
- String cheese
- Hummus and pita chips

LUNCH/SNACK

- Frozen fruit bars
- Trail Mix
- Fruit Salad
- Mini Muffins
- Yogurt cups
- Veggies with ranch dressing dip
- Mini bagels with cream cheese
- Cottage cheese topped with fruit

Real-life Example:

We've had parents bring in banana bread, a fruit salad or blueberry muffins that they've made with their child. Other times, parents have brought in mini bagels and cream cheese or carrot sticks and ranch dressing. If you are at a loss for ideas, search the Internet. Many nutritionists will offer ideas for healthy snacks for children. One of these individuals is Leanne Ely. She offers a newsletter on healthy eating and in one of her newsletters she listed 40 healthy snack ideas for children, which can be found at: www.savingdinner.com/news/40HealthySnacksForKids.html

#87 Let's Celebrate

Key Point:

When your child's birthday comes around talk to the teachers. Most of them are happy to accommodate you and make time for a simple celebration.

Summary:

If you want to have a little celebration for your child's birthday at school, please talk to the teachers about it a week or two in advance so they can plan it into the schedule. Most places will gladly accommodate you and make time for a simple celebration. No presents included of course, just maybe a special treat and activity.

Why this is Important:

When you are planning a simple party at school for your child, the teachers prefer that you bring in cupcakes rather than a cake. Children at this age do not wait patiently and they get very frustrated waiting for the teachers to cut and pass out a cake. Cupcakes can be passed out quickly to all the children making it easier and more time efficient. When planning your child's birthday celebration, ask the teachers if anyone in the class has a food allergy. If someone has a food allergy, you need to plan accordingly. Maybe you can bring in something that is okay for everyone to eat or you can call that child's

WE RECOMMEND:

WHERE THE WILD THINGS ARE

STORY AND PICTURES BY MAURICE SENDAK

Where the Wild Things Are
by Maurice Sendak
Publisher: HarperCollins

parent and give them a heads up so they know in advance about the party and will have something special for their child to eat. That way no one feels left out. If you want to bring in small party bags for the children, most schools won't mind. However, they will ask that you write each child's name on the outside of the bag and then put them in the children's cubbies. At the end of the day, the children can take them home and open them. Otherwise, someone will be sad if they lose what you gave them before it makes it home.

Real-life Example:

Some parents have provided lunch that day by bringing in pizza, juice, and cupcakes. Having a little something at school will make the child feel special and then you won't have to worry about putting on a large gathering with the group on another day!

#88 Let's Not Do Lunch

Key Point:

Make sure the teaching and support staff does not share their lunch with your child. Let the staff know you would like to be the one to introduce new foods to your child.

Summary:

You may want to talk to the teachers in advance and let them know that you would like to be the only one to introduce new foods to your child or that you would like your child to eat ONLY what is packed for him or her in their lunchbox. Upon eating a new food, some children are found to have had severe food allergies, or show intolerance to certain foods. Needless to say, whatever your wishes, make sure you discuss them with the teacher. That way they will be passed down to all who care for your child and it lessens the risk of anyone giving some of their food to your child.

Why this is Important:

Children use their five senses all day long and lunchtime is no exception. When the children are sitting down to eat, sometimes they are drawn towards someone else's food. Many well-meaning individuals, just wanting to make the child happy, may give in to a child's request and give them a little bit of their food. However, this creates lots of problems. First and foremost is the risk of food allergies. Second, these teachers may not be aware of special family practices such as a restricted diet, a kosher diet, or a vegetarian diet.

Real-life Example:

Through the years we have witnessed teachers sharing their food with the children. We always found this especially disturbing when it involved infants. One day we cringed when we saw a spoonful of eggplant going into a 10-month old baby's mouth! We know that some of you want to closely monitor any new foods introduced into your child's diet. If you do, then please be sure to specify this to the director as well as your child's teachers.

LUNCH/SNACK

#89 Chill Out!

Key Point:

Check to see if there are refrigerators available at school. If not, ice packs can be placed in your child's lunch box to keep things cold.

Summary:

Daycare centers manage snack and lunch activity differently which means the way food storage is managed will likely be different too. At any rate, you will have to find out what the deal is. If your center does not have storage for cold items, simply place ice packs in your child's lunchbox, as it will certainly keep things chilled until lunchtime. Some parents will freeze their child's juice box and use that as an ice pack as it will gradually melt and be ready to drink with lunch.

Why this is Important:

When you are looking at schools for your child, one of the things you need to do is to ask if there is a refrigerator in your child's classroom to keep their lunch cold. Some schools may only have a refrigerator in the infant/toddler area to keep the bottle and breast milk fresh. Other schools may have a refrigerator in each classroom. Other schools may only have one refrigerator, which is used to keep only the snack items that they serve from spoiling. If you discover that your child's classroom does not have a refrigerator, you'll need to pick up some ice packs.

Real-life Example:

We've never worked in one, but know of some daycare centers that have a full kitchen and chef on staff to provide both lunch and snacks. Not bad huh? These tend to be the exception and not the rule. Once you find out what the practices are for your child's center, you can plan accordingly to make sure your child has what they need for both lunch and snack time.

DAYCARE Did You Know

Over 13 million parents had children in daycare in 2012.

(Source: Department of Education; National Center for Education Statistics)

Oh Sweet Slumber!

Ok folks, this is a biggie! After all the hustle and bustle of the day, this down time is surely needed by everyone! Here you will find tips to make rest time a calming, relaxing and comfortable experience.

#90 Siesta Time

Key Point:

Wouldn't we all benefit from a little shut-eye in the middle of the day? Let children enjoy this luxury while they can. Even if they don't actually sleep, the relaxation time is good for them and helps avoid the end of the day "crankies."

Summary:

It's important to remember that "nap" is not a four-letter word. Yeah we know; you are afraid that if they sleep you will struggle getting them to sleep at night. Let's not forget, these are little people and they do require some down time in their day and don't let anyone tell you any differently. Naptime is a necessity in a childcare center as both children and teachers get a chance to calm down.

Why this is Important:

Most parents work out of necessity, which means their child may be in daycare for 8 – 9 hours a day, sometimes a little bit longer. Since these young children have such long days, most state licensing agencies require that children have a rest period, at least 1 – 1 ½ hours a day. There are parents who will ask the teachers to keep their child awake, and other parents who will tell their child not to rest. This only creates problems for everyone, especially the child who is hearing two different sets of instructions. When naptime rolls around, the children have had such a busy day that when they lay their heads down on the cot, they drift right off to sleep.

Without the break, children are going to be over tired and that can lead to emotional outbursts or cause behavior problems.

Real-life Example:

We have seen children struggling to stay awake because their mom or dad told them to. Putting your child in this confusing situation just isn't a good idea.

#91 Keep It Simple

Key Point:

Since storage space is limited in most facilities, try to provide your child with a "Nap Mat": a small blanket and pillow attached to padding they can sleep on.

Summary:

When it comes to naptime storage, space is at a premium. Most facilities struggle with storing all the cots and usually do not supply linens or pillows for your child. If this is true of your daycare center, a nap mat is ideal. This is a pillow and small blanket that are attached to padding. It rolls up easily and has Velcro to keep it rolled, making it self-contained.

Why this is Important:

When the cots are not in use, they are typically stacked on top of each other. Cots get a lot of use and are a breeding ground for germs. The nap mat helps avoid contact with germs. Try to avoid large, bulky naptime items. If you do not have or cannot find a nap mat, we recommend that you bring in a small blanket, a twin-sized sheet, and a small airline-sized pillow. Most schools will give you a small bin or a small sack to place all your child's naptime items in it. Children will be responsible for putting away their own naptime items each afternoon. So, if you are struggling to make it fit when you bring it in, then it will cause your child great frustration when they have to put it away on their own.

Real-life Example:

There have been times when children arrive with enough bedding to stay the week! Your son or daughter may want to bring in a special blanket and pillow, but practicality needs to win here. If all the kids did this, there would be no room to sleep.

> **"**
> *Rest is a part of creativity. In a culture that praises busyness, rest is an act of bravery."*
>
> **Jon Acuff**

#92 Visit the Laundry

Key Point:

Remember to bring your child's bedding home at least once per week to wash. This cuts down on the spread of germs especially during cold and flu season.

Summary:

Your child's bedding will certainly need a little freshening up after being tossed around and landing in who knows what; not to mention being stepped on, drooled on. You get the visual, no need to say anything more. Ha!

Why this is Important:

Children this age have yet to build up a strong immunity to germs, and often get sick a lot in their preschool years. They lay their heads down on their pillows and sometimes pull their blankets up to their lips; by washing the items they sleep with you will drastically cut down on the germs they are exposed to. When a child is coming down with an illness, they may not show any signs that they are getting sick, but they may be spreading their germs as they touch their blankets and pillows and those of their friends around them. Consequently, it is better to get in the habit of bringing home all your child's nap items at the end of each week to thoroughly clean them. This is especially important during cold and flu season.

Real-life Example:

We don't have a real life example for this tip. The reason is we've never encountered a parent who didn't take our advice about cleaning their child's naptime bedding. You don't want to be the first, do you? Ha!

#93 Slumber Pal

Key Point:

A favorite stuffed animal may help your child have a more comfortable and restful afternoon nap. Don't forget to bring it home at night, though. It could make for a long evening.

Summary:

Children often have one favorite stuffed toy that is their source of comfort and they carry it with them everywhere. Most likely this will be the favorite item that your child chooses to bring to school for naptime as well.

Why this is Important:

If you have children, you know what a battle it can be to get them to take a nap or go to bed. And as adults don't we always think, "just wait until you grow up - you'll be wishing you could have a nap!" Ha! Right? Anyway, it can certainly help children to settle in a little easier for naptime if you send in a favorite bedtime "blankie" or stuffed animal. For infants and young toddlers, it can be that all-important pacifier! Just seeing the object signals time to relax and can give security and comfort.

STORY TIME

We had one little boy in our class that began having nightmares during naptime. Each time, we woke him up and comforted him and tried to get him to tell us about his dream, but he never wanted to talk about it. When his father arrived at the school, the teacher informed him that his son had awakened during naptime from a nightmare. The dad thanked the teacher, collected his son's belongings and left.

We knew that this little boy's mother had lost her battle to cancer just 6 months prior, but he seemed to be handling that well. The teacher didn't know what was causing the nightmare and his father hadn't informed the teachers of any sleeping problems while at home.

For the next couple of days the same thing happened. Each time this happened, the teacher would mention it to the father, but the father still never mentioned how his son's sleep was at home. Then, one day the father came in and expressed his concerns. He said his son wasn't getting much sleep at home either and that he was always waking up in fright. The teacher told the dad just to keep reminding his son that he is safe and they will do the same at school.

Over the next couple of days, whenever the child woke from the nightmare the teacher would reassure him that he was safe and that she wouldn't let anything happen to him. Then one day, the little boy asked, "How can you do that?" The teacher wasn't sure what he was referring to, so she asked, "What do you mean...how can I do that?" And the child said, "How can you keep me safe?" When the teacher was momentarily speechless, the little boy continued to say, "Dad was watching the news last night and they said another little girl is gone, her mommy and daddy can't find her. My brother said they talked about it at his school. My brother asked me what I would do if someone took me. How will I get home?"

The teacher was so relieved that they had some idea of what was causing this little boy's nightmares and she began to reassure him as best she could. She reminded him that he was never alone and while he was at school both of his teachers would make sure he was safe and then she reminded him that the school had a fence to protect everyone. She told him that his daddy came every day to pick him up from school and sometimes even his nana and papa came to get him, but no one else. Lastly, she told him that she was glad to know what he was worried about and she would let his daddy know too. When the teacher had a free moment, she took the time to phone the little boy's father.

The father said he wasn't even aware that his son was listening to the news.

When the father arrived that night, he squatted down and hugged his son and said, "I want you to know that I would never let anyone take you. I will always protect you. If you ever get scared or worried about anything, please let me know." The little boy went home that night smiling.

We had learned that he had also talked about his fears to the other children in the class, which caused them to worry too. We informed all the parents what was happening so that they could talk to their child in their own way to lessen their fears.

Within days, this little boy was having peaceful sleep again and returned to his old happy self.

One word of caution here though; make sure you remember to bring it back home everyday. Otherwise it could mean a long evening for you!

Real-life Example:

There have been numerous times when a stuffed animal never made it home for the weekend, causing all kinds of grief for the family. Usually it's the result of rushing out the door at the end of the day and simply forgetting to check if the stuffed animal is packed up with all the other things heading home.

#94 There's a Monster Under My Bed

Key Point:

If your child is having sleep issues such as nightmares, fear of the dark, or lack of sleep, please mention this to the caregivers. Perhaps together you can arrive at some possible solutions.

Summary:

As you know yourself, lack of or disturbed sleep can lead to irritable behavior as well as a lack of energy. Once the teachers know that your child isn't sleeping, they will be more understanding and may even suggest to the child that they rest in the quiet corner or pack up their lunch and go lie down on their cot if they need to.

Why this is Important:

If your child is having sleep issues, please mention this to the caregivers. Knowing that the child is not sleeping tells the teachers a lot. Otherwise, without this information, the teacher would be concerned if they see the child acting out of character. When a child is not sleeping, it is hard for them to function in their busy day, or maneuver emotionally through the many social challenges they are faced with on a daily basis. Often, they just break down and cry.

Real-life Example:

Through the years, parents have told us about things that have worked to help alleviate nighttime fears. One mom placed a flashlight next to her daughter in bed and said that if she thought there was something in her room she should just flash the light and it would disappear. Another parent gave her son a light up wand that he was to use when the "monsters" came around. We have also found that children enjoy the books 'There's Something in My Attic' and "There's a Nightmare in My Closet" by Mercer Mayer. In these stories the children turn the tables on the scary things. Another thing we have suggested that

WE RECOMMEND:

THERE'S A NIGHTMARE IN MY CLOSET

written and illustrated by MERCER MAYER

There's a Nightmare in my Closet
By Mercer Mayer
Publisher: Puffin

has been successful is the "Monster B Gone Spray" that you and your child can make together by simply filling a spray bottle with a little fine glitter and water and just spray those nasties away! The point is to let the child feel empowered and in control of the things that go bump in the night.

#95 The Naptime Getaway

Key Point:

If you need to pick up your child during naptime, please inform the staff as soon as possible so they can get your child ready without disturbing the other children.

Summary:

If you plan on picking your child up during nap, please let the staff know this when you drop off that morning. Accommodations can then be made to assure your child is awake and ready to go without disturbing the rest of the sleeping children.

Why this is Important:

Once the staff know your child is leaving during naptime, they will gather all your child's belongings: any important notes, artwork, lunch box, backpack as well as any coat or sweater they may have brought that day. This way, when you arrive, you can easily collect everything and be on your way and there will be minimum distraction to those children that are resting. When you don't let the teachers know ahead of time, it makes it more difficult. Since the room is darkened, parents that come in at that time to get their child often have to stumble around in the dark trying to

locate all their child's things. This can be very disturbing to the children and the staff.

Real-life Example:

We can't tell you how many times a parent has promised to arrive during naptime, say at 1:00 and then doesn't show up until 2:00. As a result, we end up with an anxious child who will continually ask where his parent is, or a child who gets bored and antsy. Not exactly a fun time for all. If you are planning to arrive during naptime, but end up running late, please let the staff know as soon as possible.

See You Tomorrow!

The hours spent at daycare are now coming to a close. Getting your child to leave can sometimes be a challenge. They're tired after their busy day, too! We'll share tips for you to keep in mind as you pick up your child and make your way home.

#96 End of Day Crank

Key Point:

Do not be discouraged if your child is cranky when you pick him or her up at the end of the day. They've had a busy day and want to go home, too.

Summary:

Okay, so you know that after 8 hours of work sometimes you can be tired and maybe even a little irritable depending on the kind of day you've had. Well, the same goes for your little ones who have spent 8 or even 10 hours at childcare. They have had a full day of activities and their share of little trials and tribulations and are ready to pack it in, too. It's not always easy being a part of a group all day. So please don't get discouraged if your child seems a bit cranky at the end of their long day.

Why this is Important:

As adults, we know how hard it can be to deal with conflicts between friends and co-workers, but we've had a lifetime to practice. For children, some of the hardships that they deal with on a daily basis can be emotionally draining for them. As teachers, we can't always step

forward and rescue them or they will be ill-prepared to handle a situation when the teachers are not around. While they are in preschool, they need to be allowed to practice their social skills with a teacher close by to help, if the need should arise. However, by the end of the day some of the children will be physically drained from playing so hard and emotionally drained from dealing with each conflict that arose throughout the day and they just need to go home to relax.

Real-life Example:

We knew a dad who was an absolute "pro" with the end of day cranks. He would look at his child and very calmly state, "well boy, guess you've had enough. It's time to git outta here." And with that said, he would scoop up his son and march on out as he gave the teachers a salute.

#97 The Burning Questions

Key Point:

If you have questions about your child's day, please try to come just a few minutes earlier than your scheduled pick-up time. You'll have questions and we want to provide answers, but it's difficult if there is limited time, and many parents inquiring all at the same time.

Summary:

We know that getting information at the end of the day can sometimes be difficult as the main teachers in the classroom may have already left for the day and maybe someone who just arrived mid-afternoon is now there and doesn't have all the information you may want. This can be frustrating for sure. Some programs write out short reports that give you an idea of how your child's day went, this is true of almost all infant and young toddler areas but not always the case for preschoolers. You could always write down your concerns and address them in the morning.

Why this is Important:

If you would like to talk to your child's teacher to find out how their day was, please come in a few minutes earlier than your scheduled pick-up time to talk to them. You may want to know certain things about your child's day. Did they eat well? Did anything in particular upset them? Was he or she injured? These are all questions that parents like to know so they can start a conversation with their child about their day. However, please remember, if you arrive late and then want to talk to the teachers, you may not get all the information you are looking for. The teacher may be rushed trying to get all the end of the day chores done in order to get out on time.

Real-life Example:

If you are having issues or particular concerns with your child, one method that works well for daily communication is starting a notebook. You write in the notebook every day and hand it off to the teachers. The teachers then respond to your question or concern and can write a quick blurb about your child's day that you can pick up and read that night.

#98 We're Late for an Important Date

Key Point:

This is a biggie folks! Please make every effort to show up on time to pick up your child. It has been a very full and busy day and everyone is ready to head for home.

Summary:

Of course we all have our days where we can't get it together or things happen to cause us to be tardy and that is to be expected. However, when it happens 3 or more times a week, then there's an issue. If you are really struggling to get out of your workplace on time, talk it over with the director and maybe you can come up with a solution. Honestly, by the end of the day, the teachers are ready to go. And it's common for staff to make appointments after hours.

Why this is Important:

This is important for so many reasons. Most states require the teachers to have a certain number of continuing education hours each year. Some educational workshops or seminars take place after work hours. When the parents are on time picking up their children, the teachers usually have just enough time to get dinner and then make it to the workshop on time. However if a parent is late, then the teacher may have to forego dinner in order to make it to the workshop on time. Another consideration is that when you are late you're child watches all of their friends leave and begins to wonder where you are. Finally, by not running on time, you may be making the teacher late for his or her own personal responsibilities.

Real-life Example:

We can remember being at a function one day and overhearing a father say, "Oh I can pick up my kids a little later, I pay enough!" That comment truly demonstrates a lack of understanding and an inconsiderate attitude. Don't be that guy.

#99 Leaving is Not an Option

Key Point:

Establishing a routine when it's time to leave daycare at the end of the day is the best way to avoid a struggle with your child. For example, gather your child's things and announce, "It's time to go." Don't ask them if they are ready. Leaving is not an option.

Summary:

Avoid struggling with your child by having a routine. It's best to come in and say hello and tell your child to clean up and then it is time to leave. When ready you firmly state that it is time to go. Don't ask them if they are ready to go. Putting it in a question form gives them an option and leaving is not an option, now is it?

Why this is Important:

Establish a routine from day one and then do not deviate from it. If you show your child consistency, then they will know what to expect and they will follow through. However, some children will try to test their limits when they know that you are tired or feeling guilty for having to leave them all day long. If you give in, even once, they will test you again and again making it

come on I wanna get out of here!

difficult for you to get your child to go home without some kind of drama.

Real-life Example:

Oh, the child that does not want to leave! We have seen everything from breaking away from the parent and running amok all over the building to the child running in the parking lot refusing to get into the car. Typically it's the same children who will pull this every single night because they have been allowed to and it's just a game after a while. The conversation bubble above the teacher's head is saying, "come on I wanna get out of here!" LOL! And there stands the parent watching in dismay acting as if they have no control over the situation. Well, of course you do!

#100 Weather or Not

Key Point:

If you do not go to work or are let out early due to inclement weather conditions, please be courteous enough to keep your child home or pick them up as early as possible.

Summary:

Most childcare providers find it hard to understand why some parents do not take bad weather warnings seriously. If you can't make it for some reason, have someone on your emergency list help out. Please heed bad weather warnings and let everyone get home safe and sound!

Why this is Important:

If the daycare calls you and informs you they are closing early, please try to get to the school as soon as possible to get your child. During inclement weather, you cannot predict the driving conditions, and when you do not get to the school in a timely manner you are putting everyone else who needs to be on the road in harm's way. Even though you may live close to your child's school, the majority of the staff do not and they would like to get home safely, too. It is not unusual when major weather is predicted, that individuals who live the furthest away will opt to take a personal day and stay safely at home rather than venturing into a storm or dangerous driving conditions. As a result, your child's teacher may not be in and the school may be forced to combine classrooms to meet teacher/child regulations.

WE RECOMMEND:

Glad Monster Sad Monster
By Ed Emberley and Anne Miranda

Real-life Example:

Unfortunately we have had to risk traveling in some pretty harsh conditions. The worst was when a major hurricane was heading our way and we began evacuating the center. There was a mass exodus, but then there was only one little guy left. Believe it or not, we could not locate his parents. The mom finally showed just as the storm was starting to hit. Talk about risking lives! On yet another occasion we were being warned of an approaching blizzard and the governor was calling a state of emergency. Once again, a lone child held up closing the facility leaving two of us to stay behind. In the end, one of us had to stay at the home of someone who lived close by. The thing is, the majority of parents will be considerate of weather and act accordingly and we thank all of you for that! But, it only takes one to cause all sorts of issues.

#101 Special Event Prep

Key Point:

If you want to have your child cleaned up and changed into new clothes when taking him or her out for something special, please arrive early. The staff may not have time to do this and may even forget.

Summary:

Sometimes you may have to run right from daycare to a special event and would like your child cleaned up and put into a special outfit. If that's the case, it's better if you try to come a little earlier rather than depend on the staff to do it. It may be that the children are outside at that time or some other special activity may be going on where it's difficult for one teacher to leave to do this. And hey, yes sometimes we do forget if we get involved in something.

Why this is Important:

If you have a special after school event planned with your child like going to a sibling's school for a play or event, or starting a new after-school activity such as dance, karate or some kind of sport, don't assume the teacher can get your child ready. By the end of the day, as the children begin to go home, there might not be an extra teacher or staff member to lend a helping hand.

Don't assume, just because you brought your child's change of clothes in that they will be changed and ready to go. To be on the safe side, arrive earlier than expected. That way you will see if the teacher was able to help you out by getting your child ready. If not, you will have enough time to do it yourself.

Real-life Example:

In the past we have gladly assisted children in getting ready to go to a dance class or some other event. If the child is older, they eventually learn to get dressed all by themselves! A little note here: It's probably best not to send them in wearing their Sunday best and ask them to remain clean until you pick them up. Ha! The likelihood of that happening is slim to none.

?

DAYCARE Did You Know
About 11 million children under age 5 spend an average of 35 hours a week in child care. (source: journalistsresource.org)

#102 Tidy Time

Key Point:

If you arrive to pick up your child during clean up time, be sure your child has done his or her share of tidying up before leaving.

Summary:

A big thank you to all you folks who look at your child and say, "Do you have to put some toys away before we leave?" That is very thoughtful! It really is a good idea to make sure your little one has done his or her share of tidying up before running out the door, especially since the staff works really hard at reinforcing this task throughout the day.

> **"** *Good habits formed at youth make all the difference."*
>
> Aristotle

Why this is Important:

When your child is busy creating or playing with something they are responsible for cleaning up those things. All the children know this rule and for the most part will abide by it. However when they see their parent, they suddenly believe that this rule no longer applies to them and quickly leave to avoid cleaning up the toys they were using. It's up to you to make sure your child has cleaned up before they leave. For example, if you see your child in the block corner when you arrive, all you have to say is, "I need you to put away your blocks now." However, if you do not know what your child is responsible for cleaning, just ask the teacher. Even if your child is playing in an area with other children, they still need to clean up their share. Otherwise, once your child leaves for the day and the other children need to clean up they become angry or tearful feeling overwhelmed at the task at hand knowing they didn't create it on their own. Lastly, be careful when you rush hurriedly into the classroom to get your child and then say to them, "Come on, we got to go!" They understand this simple statement as if you were giving them permission not to clean up after themselves.

Real-life Example:

We had one clever little boy who basically knew when his dad would arrive. Moments before the dad arrived, he would dump a big bucket of toys to play with then, with a big grin on his face, he would jump into daddy's arms when he showed up. Well, we're not the new kids on the block when it comes to daycare. We caught on to that little maneuver darn quick! Before long we had him picking up his mess 10 minutes before his dad would arrive. Nice try though!

#103 Tardy Can Be Costly

Key Point:

Most daycare centers charge a fee if you arrive after closing to pick up your child. Please, acknowledge you are tardy and pay without a staff member asking.

Summary:

So, it's time to talk about the dreaded late fee. We get it: it's not always easy to arrive on time to get your child; things like traffic jams are unavoidable. However, most places have a late policy that needs to be enforced to encourage habitual tardy people to show up on time. Each center has a different way of handling late fees so please be sure to check the policy book to see what the procedure is.

Why this is Important:

Each time a parent is late, state law usually requires that two teachers must stay with that child until the parent's arrival. When the school closes, these teachers may have other commitments of their own to get to; whether that is to get home to their own families, to go to school, or they may have to get to another job. Although most of these teachers often have a degree in Early Childhood Education or a related field, their salary is by no means comparative to that of an Elementary school teacher even though they are responsible for teaching these children what they need to know in order to prepare them for Kindergarten. Make yourself aware of the late policy and the consequences there of. Some schools have a monetary fee for tardiness. Other schools may have a stricter "zero-tolerance" policy, which means you will be asked to find another school for your child to accommodate your late hours. Lastly, please acknowledge you are tardy and pay the fee without a staff member asking you for it. Discussing

money issues can be uncomfortable, but staff will ask you for the late fee if they have to.

Real-life Example:

We have worked for daycare centers where there was no late policy and we were sometimes there for half an hour after closing. It made it very difficult to make appointments or plans for after work. Remember, teachers are people, too!

#104 Pack 'em Up

Key Point:

As your child gets older, make them an active part of gathering their belongings into a backpack to take home. Children need this guidance for a year, before they go to kindergarten and are expected to be responsible for this task on their own.

Summary:

During the last year that your child is at preschool, guide them at pick-up time to put on their sweater or coat, put their own backpack on their back and carry their own lunchbox. By being responsible for all of their belongings through your guidance, they will be able to be responsible for this task on their own in kindergarten.

> **"**
> *Children must be taught how to think, not what to think."*
>
> **Margaret Mead**

Why this is Important:

The daycare center's role is to prepare children for kindergarten. Each day, when the parent drops off their child or even picks them up, we observe the parents schlepping in with all of their child's belongings while the child skips or runs alongside them. What parents do not realize is that by taking care of all their child's things and not making them responsible for something, they will be ill prepared to do it on their own when they move onto kindergarten. The key is to gradually make them responsible to carry something of their own. Once they are older and can understand a command, ask them to carry their lunchbox or something that needs to be brought into the school or home. Once children get even a little older, purchase them a small backpack and begin to teach them that they need to put everything into that, so that it can go home. Remind them that after lunch or afternoon snack, they need to put the lunchbox into the backpack. Let them know that after nap their stuffed toy needs to go into the backpack as well or it will be forgotten. At first, your child most likely won't remember. Do not step in and automatically do it all for them. This teaches them nothing. You'll need to guide them for a little until they are doing it on their own without prompting. When you come into the school and you find that your child's backpack is all packed up and ready to go, then you will know that they are on their way to mastering this task.

Real-life Example:

As adults, we tend to try to do everything we can for the children, especially the ones under three. But a mom once gave us some wise advice when she came back for a visit after her child left for kindergarten. She expressed that she wished she had encouraged her little girl to be more responsible for packing up her belongings to get her into the habit of taking care of and remembering all her things at school. I guess many items were left behind at the end of the day!

#105 Bravo! Bravo!

Key Point:

If your child is having a very difficult time leaving, you may have to step forward and physically pick them up. Don't be afraid the teachers are judging you. They will applaud your assertiveness.

Summary:

Oh the struggles you can have getting your little one out of the building and even into the car to get home! So, if your child is having a difficult time leaving, you may have to calmly step forward and physically pick them up. Don't ignore the behavior or it will persist. Don't be afraid the teachers are judging you; they will applaud your assertiveness.

Why this is Important:

There are times when a parent arrives to pick up their child and their child begins to act up and won't leave. Sometimes, rather than speaking to their child, they give them some leeway. Parents have said they do this for many reasons:

▪ They feel guilty that they have to work and then leave their child in childcare.

▪ They don't want to draw attention to the situation and their child's behavior.

▪ They don't want to turn it into a game of cat and mouse by having to chase their child around the school.

▪ They don't want to embarrass themselves.

Whatever the reason, some parents do not react the first time their child displays this behavior and therefore it happens again and again. Sometimes it even creates a domino effect. When one child sees another child behaving badly and getting attention for it, they may begin to give their parent a hard time too. Avoid the mayhem. Assert yourself and be consistent.

Real-life Example:

A toddler had grown accustomed to gleefully running around the building away from his mom and dad every time they came to pick him up. And yes there were bribes and promises, threats, and demands, but the little guy just kept running. The thing is, in a case like this, you may have to just step forward and pick up the child kicking and screaming and walk out the door. We know as a parent you may feel like the teachers are judging you and that resorting to physical means may be frowned upon. Quite the contrary my dear parent, we will be applauding your assertiveness!

A Community of Parents

 Parents of children in daycare have come together and joined the Dear Daycare Parent online community. Membership is free and provides parents with access to special offers from our growing list of partners, and other benefits including important information, special invitations to in-person and virtual events, and Q&A sessions with the authors.

The only requirements for membership are your sincere interest in making daycare great for your children and the children of others, a valid e-mail address, permission to send you our e-mail newsletter, and any offers we make available to you from our partners.

To join, visit www.deardaycareparent.com and click on Community.

Thank you for your support of our work and for making the daycare experience great!

Jacqueline N. Rioux

Jackie Rioux has been in the child development field for over twenty-five years, most recently with Knight Hall School in West Hartford, Connecticut where their tradition of delivering a quality child-care experience, since 1929, is still in practice. Prior to joining Knight Hall, Jackie served as Assistant Director of the preschool at the former world-renowned Newington Children's Hospital in Newington, Connecticut.

Her vast experience includes all phases of the child-care industry including starting daycare and pre-school programs from scratch. She has had much success in creating learning and cognitive development programs throughout her career and is widely recognized as a leader in her field.

Jackie holds a B.A. in Child Development from Central Connecticut State University.

Jo-Ann Parylak

Jo-Ann Parylak has over twenty years of experience in early childhood education, working most recently at Knight Hall School in West Hartford, Connecticut, where teachers such as Jo-Ann help foster learning in a non-competitive, loving environment. Prior to joining Knight Hall, Jo-Ann served as a preschool teacher at the Newington Children's Hospital in Newington, Connecticut.

During her ten-year career at Newington, Jo-Ann fostered a reputation as a creative storyteller. She is a member of four storytelling organizations: The League for the Advancement of New England Storytelling, The Connecticut Storytelling Association, The National Storytelling Association, and the Healing Story Alliance.

Today, Jo-Ann uses her passion for storytelling in her work as a reading tutor for children. She also spent over a decade teaching adults to read as a volunteer with Literacy Volunteers of Greater Hartford.

Jo-Ann received her A.S. in Early Childhood Education from Greater Hartford Community College, now known as Capital Community College, in Hartford, Connecticut.